# UNCEILING YOUR CAREER

# UNCEILING YOUR CAREER

Natalie H. Luke, PhD

NEW DEGREE PRESS
COPYRIGHT © 2022 NATALIE LUKE
*All rights reserved.*

UNCEILING YOUR CAREER

ISBN  979-8-88504-822-4  *Paperback*
      979-8-88504-933-7  *Kindle Ebook*
      979-8-88504-588-9  *Ebook*

*For my mother and hero, Beverly Heinking; my best friend, accountability partner, supporter, and husband, Tom Luke; and my talented loving daughter, Megan Luke.*

# Contents

INTRODUCTION . . . . . . . . . . . . . . . 9

CHAPTER 1. INVISIBLE BARRIERS . . . . . . . . . . . . 19

CHAPTER 2. YOUR UNIQUE DESTINY . . . . . . . . . . . 33

CHAPTER 3. CREATING A POSITIVE VISION . . . . . . . . 47

CHAPTER 4. BREAKING THE CYCLE . . . . . . . . . . . . 59

CHAPTER 5. STEP FORWARD AND KEEP MOVING . . . . . 69

CHAPTER 6. STAND UP AND BRAG! . . . . . . . . . . . . 79

CHAPTER 7. ANALYZING PAST SUCCESSES PRODUCES INCREASED CONFIDENCE . . . . . . . . . . 93

CHAPTER 8. NETWORKING-CONNECTING VISIONS . . . 103

CHAPTER 9. DEALING WITH SETBACKS . . . . . . . . . 113

CHAPTER 10. PULLING IT ALL TOGETHER . . . . . . . . 125

ACKNOWLEDGMENTS . . . . . . . . . . . 135

APPENDIX . . . . . . . . . . . . . . . . . 137

# Introduction

---

"The journey to success is as important as the destination."

Beverly told me, "'Women should not be allowed to drive!'"

"What?" Shocked, angry, and astonished, I asked with my eyes furiously narrowed and my lips pursed.

"Yup! Can you believe it? My parents wouldn't allow me to learn how to drive a car simply because I was a girl!" Beverly introspectively remembered when asked how she became a physician in her thirties during an era most women wouldn't dream of attending medical school.

Beverly is my mother. My mother's parents insisted she not learn how to drive, but she did anyway. Against the rules, Mom bought a car and drove her way into becoming a practicing physician and my hero.

Driving was just one of the glass barriers she shattered. How did she buck authority figures and break those barriers? Mom had a secret way about her. Time and time again, I watched Mom take action and trust herself, her abilities, and her intuitive voice.

Looking back on her accomplishments, I figured out Mom's secret sauce of transforming her life and our family's future for the better. I also discovered how I've employed the process and it, too, has improved our families' lives.

We could all employ Mom's secret sauce because we women must all buck the system. The demonstrated fact that women are often the minority in leadership roles in our patriarchal society is evidence of needing to oppose the established rules. Our patriarchal society has a set of specific guidelines on how we, as women, should define ourselves. Having confidence in ourselves, abilities, and intuitive voices can be challenging. Women have an expectation placed upon them to look and behave in a manner that is agreeable to the beliefs of the community in which they live (Itty, 2019).

In many ways, women are held back from being the confident individuals they could be due to the narrow ideas of what women should be and what they should do in the world. The self-confidence gap begins in adolescence and remains with each of us for the rest of our lives, no matter the country in which we reside (Blieborn, 2016). As a result of the self-confidence gap, our wages are lower, our career opportunities are reduced, and fewer women own their own businesses. In fact, women are only 21 percent of entrepreneurs who start companies then receive only 10 percent of all venture capital funding (Guzman, 2019).

The strict rules society places on us cause us to have perfectionist tendencies. These traditional rules dictate that we are not qualified for leadership roles unless we check off a series of boxes or if an authority figure taps us on the shoulder. Perfectionism leads to strict, black-and-white demands on us that further reduce our faith in ourselves. This often causes us to falsely believe we are unprepared for leadership roles or do not possess skills that will enable us to take on challenging and demanding projects.

Furthermore, our perfectionist inclinations cause us to place unrealistic expectations on ourselves, such as the obligation to always say yes or never take credit for our efforts or positive job results. All these things further contribute to the erosion of our self-assurance.

I propose that because of a lack of faith in ourselves, we are missing out on a vision of how our lives could be.

Many of us grew up with a scarcity mindset, which causes us to doubt our own abilities. If an authority figure doesn't tap us on the shoulder or we don't have a supportive mentor, we won't go for a bigger and better role. In this situation, we remain in mediocrity, with our potential resting dormant on the table. Alternatively, some of us take action but feel we need to work twice as hard as necessary, causing us to burn out.

My mother taught me a different way. She taught me that everything starts with a dream of a better future. Mom instilled in me the notion of dreaming big and being daring. Mom said the goal should make your palms sweat because the aim is scary but doable. The dream should be so exciting that it makes your heart sing. She taught me the importance of doing homework (planning) and then gathering the tools and people needed to achieve the dream. She showed me how to take action and work with others to make things happen.

Most importantly, she trained me to use rejection, obstacles, and failure as learning opportunities for attaining ambitions. Being perfect, checking every box, or waiting for the tap on the shoulder never entered Mom's formula, though listening to feedback did.

It took me a while to learn and enact the lessons Mom taught me. My career didn't start off as strong as I had hoped after college. Immediately after graduation, all the positive expectations, which were once high, dropped to an all-time low. I had graduated with a full scholarship for both music and science. However, against my parent's advice, I dropped out of premed and opted to start my career as a science teacher. After graduation and interviewing for high school biology or chemistry teaching roles in several school districts, I could only land a job as a substitute teacher for a year before attaining my first full-time high school instructor role.

I ended up not enjoying teaching and wasn't sure how to pivot my career. Had you told the past Natalie of the future Natalie, she may not have believed you. Past Natalie would have broken down into tears or said the notion was flat-out crazy. No way could past Natalie have imagined what current Natalie would be able to accomplish.

Today, I manage a research budget most university professors aspire to. In my current position, I lead a team to produce research papers and design clinical studies involving the world's most brilliant physicians and academic leaders. I then take the insights from the studies to assist the marketing team in educating health care providers on the most modern technologies to diagnose diseases. I also work with a group of people dedicated to developing new diagnostic tests and technologies that make a difference in patients' lives.

Who am I? My name is Natalie Luke, and today I am Vice President of Clinical Research at the company I'm currently employed. I am also a wife, a mom of a beautiful and intelligent teenage girl, a sister, and a daughter. I earned an interdisciplinary PhD in molecular biology, biochemistry, cell biology, and biophysics. I also enjoy playing tennis. I am a writer and author and an advocate for empowering women. In short, I'm lots of things.

Some people describe me as creative, energetic, and focused. Others label me a "dog with a bone" because they can count on me to stick with a strategy or task until I finish the challenging job. While I am tagged a bulldog, I have lived six of a cat's nine lives. My career transitioned from high school teacher, to graduate student, to sales professional in biotech, to director of sales, national training director, marketing director, and a director of clinical research before becoming a vice president. Most of the transitions took place while working within two companies. This means that within a corporate environment, I was able to either transfer to a new department or climb up the career ladder.

My bold career transitions wouldn't have happened without Mom's formula. I had confidence in my ability to learn, take action towards my dreams, find people who could help me, and listen and learn from others. I express myself in a way that is authentically me. My mother taught me the importance of listening to the small voice inside that says, "You can do this." As a result, like Mom, I've created a new future for myself and my family.

I decided I needed to immortalize Mom's formula after sitting in a leadership meeting and wondering, *Where is Davetta?*, or the female name for David. You're probably wondering why I would ask such a question, "Where is Davetta?" Let me explain.

At the time of this remarkable meeting, I was working for a company in which our leadership team was comprised of 50 percent women and 50 percent men, but the C-suite was made up of only men. A small percentage of the women working in the company topped out at the vice president level. At that time, I had the title of an assistant vice president. More interesting was that half of the men in the C-Suite were named David. We resorted to referring to these men by their last names to keep them straight.

When a new CEO came into the organization, we were graciously invited to meet him. We also were asked to introduce ourselves to him. The men introduced themselves first, beginning, as an example with, "My name is David Smith;

you can call me Smith." Next person, "My name is David, and you can call me by my last name." Third person, "My name is David Sam Pico," joking, and we all laughed. Sam was the third person's actual first name; however, since many of the other people's names were David, why not continue? The new CEO realized what was intuitively already known by many members of the company but never acknowledge by any of us: "Guess you can't get to the C-suite unless your name is David." The inference was clear. You had to be a man to get to the C-suite.

Upon hearing out loud what we already silently knew, I hatched a plan.

After the meeting ended, I huddled with the women who were in the room. The insinuation that you can't get to the C-suite unless you were a man didn't escape the other women either. I was very relieved to know I wasn't the only person struck by the discussion. I didn't debate the conclusion with any of the men in the meeting; I suspect the statement that "you can't get to the C-suite unless you are a man" didn't hit the male leaders as it did us. For them, it could have been a matter of fact. I'm confident the new CEO didn't know that in the past I had to point out that my name should be followed by PhD on meeting itineraries, just as my male colleagues who earned a PhD did.

After the noteworthy gathering, my plan was to find a way to elevate women in our workplace. We need women in the C-suite and more women leaders at all levels. We women must raise our leadership energy levels, the vision of ourselves, and our visibility.

To that end, I proposed the idea of starting an Empowering Women's group in the company. The organization wholeheartedly embraced the idea, both the men and the women.

I also began rewriting this book. I had written a version of this book seven years prior and released it as an e-book only. Since then, my career has grown and transitioned, adding more content to share. Additionally, researchers have produced a lot more data about how women do and don't succeed.

My intent in starting the women's leadership program and rewriting this book was to achieve three goals. First, increase my confidence; second, raise my leadership energy levels; and last, provide a framework to become my highest self. (Yes, even after all my achievements and success, I have self-doubts.) In achieving these three aims for myself, I reasoned, I would help other women also raise their level of confidence.

This book is to be a confidence-builder benefitting any woman who realizes she wishes to make a career transition or climb the career ladder.

If this is you, you will find an easy-to-follow, holistic plan to transition your life for the better. You'll find mentorship and guidance through Mom's and other women's stories, along with data from research studies presented throughout. The advice delivered in the book are things my mother had to build from scratch or had to take on faith when she started on her path to medical school.

You now have in your possession a process, stories, and tools to help you succeed. The formula will show you how to tap into your intuition and plan a vision worthy of your energy. If you've hit an obstacle, you'll find the framework to solve one problem at a time to realize your vision—just like my mother.

The formula isn't a one-and-done deal. You can use the process repeatedly as you transition from one situation to another. Life happens, and you grow. You gain perspective, leading to a change in your aspirations. You may start your career desiring challenging roles. Later, you may yearn for a little more balance. As you end your career, you may desire more stature, or you may decide you want a position that allows you to leave a legacy. As the goals for your career change, you can use the formula to adjust your next transition to fit your ambitions.

The good news is anyone can learn to trust themselves and take calculated risks. Achieving one beautiful, bold, palms-sweating vision worthy of pursuit after another is possible. I hope you can apply the stories and research information to better your career and improve your confidence.

Having confidence and taking risks is essential because those women who succeed do so by taking on various roles within the company. Their careers don't resemble the climbing of a career ladder. Instead, the career path corresponds to walking toward the center of a spider's web. We become influential leaders by trusting in our abilities and judgment, in addition to getting things done, influencing others, and feeling comfortable in our own skin. Beyond that, we must be in a supportive structure. From there, we will succeed.

You'll start your journey by identifying the "glass" that holds you back so you can shatter it without getting cut. Before breaking free of the barrier, you'll see a vision and, once you are liberated from the shards, you'll be on your way. You'll have so much confidence that when others or your own critical voice says, "You can't," you won't even hear the negative message.

When problems arise, the stories in this book can inspire you to find solutions like an agile ninja rather than stop you in your tracks. Once you learn the lessons in here, you'll use the teachings repeatedly because, after you've achieved a single success, you'll go for another. Like muscle memory, you'll not forget the process. Your life will be an inspiration for others around you, including your children. Your purpose awaits you.

Let's get started with your destiny for greatness.

Scan the QR code to access bonus items.

# CHAPTER 1

# Invisible Barriers

"Despite being bombarded by others, live life according to your values."

Mom had a way of not just breaking through barriers; she walked through glass walls as if they were not there. The rules that applied to other women seemed to not pertain to her. She began teaching me her secrets of breaking through invisible boundaries at a young age. One of her lessons took place on a weekend morning.

I thought it strange that Mom and I were driving to see Grandma independently without the rest of the family. We normally trekked to Grandma's house all together, Mom, Dad, and us three kids, but not this day.

On this warm summer day, Mom was strangely quiet as we drove the forty-five minutes it took to arrive at Grandma's house in Chicago. We lived in the suburbs outside the city, and Grandma lived in the same place in which she was born, near the downtown area and the other Lithuanians that made up her extended family.

In retrospect, I believe my mom wanted me to be with her for support, even though I was only sixteen and naive to the family dynamics that would soon come into play.

Grandma lived on the bottom floor of a two-story, one-hundred-year-old farmhouse. As we walked in the front door, we were immediately greeted by a long, dark staircase that led to an upstairs apartment and the distinct old house smell that comes from such age. Even as a teen, the dark staircase seemed scary. We had once lived in the upper dwelling when Mom and Dad were first married. I was brave enough to go up the stairs when my brother or sister was with me. No way would I venture up by myself. After entering the front door, Mom and I ignored the scary stairwell and walked through Grandma's front door.

Grandpa had died a few years earlier, causing my aunt to move in with Grandma. Even after Grandpa died, Grandma still believed women shouldn't drive, which meant that Auntie had to drive her to the store or wherever she needed to go. Now that I think about it, I find it strange that Auntie was allowed to drive, but Mom wasn't. I guess Mom bucking the rules made it easier for Auntie to buck them too.

In any case, Grandma's life was very predictable: church on Sunday, Fish Fry on Friday nights, and once a month we visit on Saturday.

I loved eating at Grandma's house because she was an excellent cook; she presented us with authentic Lithuanian food. Despite the nearly silent drive over, we had a nice, casual lunch. Grandma made us delicious egg sandwiches, the kind I loved, with sweet pickles on the side along with chips.

As we got up to leave through the living room and began heading for the front door, my mother abruptly announced, "Great news. I've been admitted to medical school. We are moving to Kansas City in the summer so I can start school in the fall."

Mom was accepted into a medical school's next class when she was thirty-one years old, at a time when fewer than 25 percent of students were women (AAMC, 2016).

I expected Grandma to be excited, just like the rest of our nuclear family. Instead, Grandma's response shocked me.

Grandma exploded. "What do you think you're doing, Bevie? You're getting older, not younger. Your brain cells die as you get older, and you get more stupid." Clearly, Grandma wasn't happy about Mom moving away to attend medical school.

I was impressed with my mom for this accomplishment, as were all those friends in my teenage circle. Grandma was unimpressed and unhappy. Grandma was genuinely fishing for any reason to dissuade my mother from moving away and going to medical school.

I turned to my mom in shock. "Really? You're getting more stupid?" I said with my mouth hanging open. I couldn't imagine Mom losing her intellect. "How would we even measure that?"

My teenage prankster mind started swirling, joking inside. I imagined how I could use Grandma's faulty logic in my favor. *Boy, Mom, you must be getting dumber as you age*, I could say to my advantage… That is, only when Mom was in a playful mood; otherwise, I'd get a slap upside the head.

Seriously, I expected Mom to be frustrated and angry at Grandma for not appreciating her achievements. Instead, my mother turned to me and softly suggested I wait outside in the car.

Mom was amazingly calm.

I realize now that I was witnessing Mom dealing with a barrier that can hold women back from reaching their full potential. In today's terms, the hidden barricades that keep women in mediocrity in the workplace are termed "glass."

Marilyn Loden first coined the term "glass ceiling" in the late seventies, and it became more widely used starting in the eighties. A "glass ceiling" is an invisible barrier that prohibits women and minorities from moving into companies' senior levels (Ganiyu, 2018).

After the term "glass ceiling" became famous, other authors invented similar "glass" concepts. There are "glass ceilings," "glass walls," "glass cliffs," "glass fences," and "glass elevators." "Glass walls" are the barriers that stop women from making lateral transitions in companies. "Glass cliffs" are ascribed to situations in which women take a challenging position as a leader (one which a man wouldn't dare) because the risk of failure is extremely high (Ryan, 2016). "Glass fences" are the invisible impediments that prohibit women from taking active positions outside the home. Fences are primarily applied to Middle Eastern and Asian cultures, where religion and society highly prescribe women's roles as being exclusively in the home (Kim, 2013).

Contrary to the glass barriers women face, some men can encounter glass too. But the "glass" men experience is different from the glass women contend with. Rather than being blocked by "glass," men are escorted to senior-level positions within organizations. The term "glass elevators" describes the fast-paced track men take when entering a field predominantly employed by women. These men are quickly shuffled to the top of the organization (Williams, 1992).

I'm not sure how Mom ended the discussion with Grandma that day. Whatever Mom said didn't persuade Grandma's thinking. Unfortunately, Grandma's disagreeable opinion about medical school didn't change. Grandma voiced her opposing opinion often and loudly.

Mom continued to deal with glass, as the news didn't land well with the other side of the family either. On Dad's side, Great-grandma was the matriarch of the family. Great-grandpa died of the Spanish flu soon after Great-grandma's third son, my grandpa, was born. With the death of Great-grandpa, Great-grandma and her children had to move back in with her parents. She then worked in the city during the week while her parents cared for her children. Great-grandma was thankful for the family's assistance during that time. The family was vital to her.

When Mom disclosed the news that we needed to relocate so she could attend medical school to Dad's side of the family, Great-grandma's fear was triggered. Having suffered such a significant loss early in life and obtaining help from her parents at such a critical time left a substantial impression on her. Great-grandma's advice about the situation was not to go. "Forget about attending medical school. Bevie, your roots are here!" Great-grandma argued. "How can you leave your family?" The extended family's rules maintained that as women, we must live geographically close to the family for protection and out of loyalty. Service to the family was important.

Each society and family has its own set of rules, which is another kind of glass that boxes us in. The societal rules impacting women vary from the belief that women should not have power, speak up, be competitive, take charge, or control situations. Instead, women should keep their heads down in the workplace. Extended from this, the rule is, don't draw attention to yourself by pointing out your hard work. Hard work gets noticed. When not at work, women should perform housework and raise children. That is their job.

Other societies, such as in Korea, believe that any labor a woman pursues is less than a man's. The logic follows, since a woman's function in the company is less significant, their pay will also be less than the man's compensation. Alternatively, the women's work supplements men's work; therefore, there is no need to pay women equally.

In the foreword of the book *Breaking the Glass Box*, Dr. Rosemary Radford Ruether explains the complexity of social rules that keep Korean women from pursuing roles outside of the home. She lists the seven rules women are to obey, including to "be obedient to her parents-in-law, to give birth to a son, not to be talkative, not to commit adultery, not to be jealous of her husband's concubine, not to carry a malignant disease, and not to commit theft. Quiet subjugation to her subordinate position in the household was a women's lot in marriage" (Yu, 2013).

Korea's silent societal rules have led to the highest pay gap between women and men relative to the rest of the world's countries (Patterson, 2020); for Korean women, there is a 37.4 percent wage difference (Hankyoreh, 2014).

An American version of the societal rule is demonstrated on a 1966 *Andy Griffith Show* episode called "Goober's Replacement." Goober's girlfriend, Flora, offered to substitute for Goober at the gas station when no one else could cover when he went on a two-week fishing trip. All the men in town thought it was cute that a woman would attempt to perform a man's job. They felt sorry for the owner because having a woman around the business would undoubtedly cause a drop in customer traffic. However, the opposite happened. Instead of slower business, Flora brought in shoppers. The gas station broke commercial records with Flora in charge.

The owner naturally favored Flora staying on board, so Goober had to find a new job. Unfortunately, Goober had a hard time. After looking for other employment, landing jobs, and being fired, Goober decided he had to find a position at a gas station outside of town.

Sheriff Andy Taylor, the main character and hero of the show, decided he needed to set things straight, and it was time to explain a few things to Flora. The sheriff joined Flora for lunch. Not knowing Goober's difficulties, Flora excitingly told the sheriff of all the ways she could grow the gas station business.

The sheriff noted Flora's excitement and acknowledged her great head for business. He then stated, "You know, most girls don't have much on their mind but about getting married. You might have your own gas station with your business head one day. I know a girl who kept working and eventually got her own store."

The sheriff explained that his female friend ended up living on her own, never married, and feeding her cats at night while studying the business numbers. There was little time else for the poor lady. Flora deduced that if she continued working at the gas station, she would never marry.

The sheriff's lesson was clear: Flora had to quit. Happily, Goober got his old job back. Mind you, I watched this show at the age of ten as I was doing housework and ironing clothes. Flora probably returned to performing household tasks while waiting for Goober to come back from work. The implications were clear to me too. I had to ask myself, "Is housework all there is in store for me? Isn't there more to learn and do?"

As I watched the show, I fully expected Flora to say, "Sorry, Sheriff, I know you love Goober, but the bottom line is that I'm better at bringing in business than him. There is no reason I need to quit. With all the business I'm bringing in, there's enough room for both of us." Instead, she quit and waited for Goober to come around for dinner now and again. I don't remember seeing Flora in any other episode.

"What happens after marriage?" I asked myself.

"Your job is to iron shirts," I imagined the sheriff would say to me with a smile.

"Ha!" I scoffed at the sheriff in my fictional version of the story. "Ironing shirts, cleaning the house, washing dishes, vacuuming. I'm only ten, and I've got all these tasks down, pat! Is that all I have to offer? Ironing shirts isn't what I want to do with my life. I want to learn, grow, and make a difference."

Okay, I give you license to believe that a ten-year-old wouldn't articulate such mature thoughts. Nevertheless, even now as an adult, I remember the episode. I can't help but see the sheriff in my mind's eye when I hear comments about a woman's place in the world.

Of course, this is only a TV show. I had a different role model. Like other parents in our neighborhood, Mom and Dad married young out of high school and immediately had three children. But Mom differed from the other mothers in town. My mom had a ton going on.

When I was six, my mom decided to start college and pursue a career in nursing. When I was about nine, Mom and Dad became business owners, eventually managing three stores jointly, with Mom taking care of the books. Together they owned a deli/liquor store and two grocery stores. Mom had time for us despite working in the stores, continuing to pursue degrees, and working in hospitals as an emergency department nurse. Mom studied with us at night and helped us with our homework.

Mom was out there working, growing, and making a difference. That's what I wanted for myself. The sheriff explained to poor Flora that she was taking a job from a man. Even if Flora had a better head for business, taking a man's job wasn't right. That was the rule being taught to us girls.

Cultural norms around the roles we should take are taught to us women in so many ways, be it through entertainment, school, and who knows what else.

"Glass" is comprised of black-and-white rules that box us in with our permission, acceptance, and lack of creativity. Societal rules and cultural norms silently teach us what it means to be the "ideal worker." In general, it's believed that women are not solely committed to work. Such a rule stands regardless of our family status, be it single, married, or with children or not: our primary aim is home and family, with no room for work. Therefore, working women will have competing priorities.

We are taught that there are men's jobs and there are women's jobs. Women shouldn't do a man's work. Lastly, women have little to offer. When women enter the workforce, their contributions are often not regarded as necessary (Hall, 2020).

One summer during college, I worked in construction, putting up fences and building decks. As you can imagine, semi-heavy labor was physically involved, and I was paid less because I couldn't carry as many boards at once or hammer as quickly as the men. But the quality of the men's work was poor and sometimes had to be redone. Unfortunately for the owner, the men refused to work overtime.

In contrast, though I was slower and couldn't carry as many boards as the men, I performed quality work and was willing to work overtime to meet demanding deadlines. One day, I noticed the men's work on the fences was of such inferior quality that the wall nearly fell. I offered to work overtime to redo their work. "Why is it," I asked the owner, when completing the job, "that you pay the men more than me, yet I'm the only one willing to stay late and repair their poor work?"

He didn't have an answer, nor would he pay me more, so I quit. That boss lost a conscientious and quality worker because he couldn't see past the black-and-white mindset that a woman can't do a man's job. True, I was slower, but I did my work right the first time and was willing to inspect it to make sure it was of the quality needed.

As part of the "glass ceilings and walls" mindset, minimizing comments also communicate a reduced respect level to women's work. Hall and associates describe several different variations of marginalizing communication styles in the workplace for women (Hall et al., 2020).

- Isolating communication: The women are physically separated from the men in this situation. Therefore, the men are privy to the information above and beyond that of the women.
- Being silenced: This is where the women's viewpoint is rejected or viewed as incompetent. Later, when a man brings up the same points, it's respected and seems heard for the first time.
- Markers of disrespect: In this situation, even when the women are more educated and experienced, they are not provided the respect they deserve or earned. Their credibility is constantly questioned.
- Violence or sexual harassment: This occurs when men feel threatened if they suspect a woman of taking his job.
- Lack of tolerance for physical needs: In these situations, women are sidelined based on an aspect of their physical appearance.

I can relate to the "markers of disrespect." As a PhD, I am meticulous when it comes to analyzing and citing data; however, in some of the companies I've worked, when I disclosed my conclusions, I was needlessly and constantly challenged. Over time, I learned to publicize my findings through a man other people respected. He in turn announced my conclusions to others, and we then moved on to the next project.

When Mom got into the car after Grandma exploded, I asked, "Is everything okay?"

Calmly, as if nothing happened, she said, "Yes, Natalie, everything is fine." As an adult, I couldn't imagine being told by my mom that I was getting dumber, especially after being accepted into medical school. I wondered what it would be like to hear my elders accuse me of disloyalty for pursuing my dreams. I would not have handled it calmly; I might have exploded or doubted myself to the point of giving up. Yet Mom was unfazed. She listened to the minimizing comments and didn't complain, sulk, or hold a grudge.

Later, I asked Mom about that period. "How did you stay calm and move forward without holding any grudges?" When the extended family admonished Mom for advancing on with her dream of being a physician, she listened as she was told she was stupid and disloyal.

Mom revealed, "I had compassion for your grandma and great-grandma. I put myself in their shoes. I thought about how I would have felt if any of you three kids needed to move away from me to pursue a dream. I may have said the same type of things to you three kids. But I knew I needed to attend medical school. It was important to our nuclear family."

Listening with compassion and not taking in outdated rules was the first step in Mom's secret method of breaking through glass without getting cut. Mom knew she was breaking the rules, and she listened to alarming accusations with compassion. While they said, "Bevie, you are getting dumber," or "Bevie, you are disloyal," she heard, "Bevie, we're going to miss you." Her secret was not to listen to the words; instead, Mom understood the emotion driving the words. Mom then equally combined her compassion for others with her passion for the vision she was moving toward achieving.

Mom gave herself room to hold two conflicting thoughts in her head and heart at one time. She had compassion for those giving minimizing messages while also focusing on an extraordinary vision for the future. Through her compassion for those who underestimated or wanted to stop her, she found a way to break glass without getting cut.

Mom never fought her elders. She listened, accepted they were afraid, and pursued her vision with or without their acceptance. Eventually, the family recognized that Mom was headed to medical school and there was nothing they could do but acknowledge it. Four years later, the same people who initially rejected the move proudly attended Mom's graduation ceremony. Mom walked through the glass wall and changed the rules for the other women in our family.

Scan the QR code to access bonus items.

## CHAPTER 2

# Your Unique Destiny

---

*"Nothing would ever get done if everyone waited until everything was perfect to get started."*

My mom would never have the perfect time to apply for medical school. If I were my mom's friend and she came to me for advice at that time, I might have actually told her that I could think of several good reasons why her dream of becoming a physician shouldn't have ever entered her mind at that point in her life.

First, Mom started applying to medical school when our family struggled financially. Mom and Dad owned two grocery stores and a deli. Two out of the three stores were successful, but the third store wasn't profitable, operating at such a financial loss that it threatened to take the other two stores down and push our family into bankruptcy. To help make ends meet, my siblings and I toiled in the stores when we were not doing school, sports, or music.

Dad slogged in the stores sixteen hours a day, seven days a week. The one defective store had my family teetering on the edge of either monetary success or fiscal ruin. We were uncertain if we would be able to sell the stores so that Mom could attend medical school. If we couldn't sell, or worse, the third store went into foreclosure, our family dreams would be lost.

Second, when my mom applied to medical school, we three kids entered junior high. We were all encouraged and had the grades and aptitude to attend college; any logical person would ask, "How will you pay for medical school and for all the kids going to college simultaneously?"

Last, in the 1980s, roughly 41,000 applicants applied to about 150 medical schools in the United States, including medical doctor (MD) and doctor of osteopathy (DO) schools. Mom learned that MD schools were not open to applicants like her: older and interested in entering medical school at the age of thirty-one. Medical schools issuing an MD were interested in younger students, which meant Mom had to target the twenty-five DO schools. Roughly four thousand students submitted applications to DO medical schools in the 1980s for one of 3,500 positions. It seemed Mom's chances of getting in were slim (AAMC, 2014).

Ironically, even though I could think of several reasons why Mom shouldn't even consider applying to medical school, she said she couldn't come up with any justifications not to attempt applying at the time.

Mom didn't let circumstances stop her. Instead, she owned her personal power and confidently moved forward with her dream. I have no idea how she learned to hold personal power, but I know what it feels like. It's as if at first, you're taking a tentative step forward, looking around for danger or a reaction, then a light switch flips and you need to do what you do with power and confidence. It's as if at first you were driving with one foot on the brake and one foot on the gas, and you decide to release the foot on the break. You go.

Unfortunately, women are often conditioned to expect and accept rejection. Meaning their foot is always on the break. This conditioning causes women to not even consider taking the initial step.

For example, I reported that medical schools were not accepting older people. It should be noted that I did not say they would not accept female students into their program. Medical schools were indeed accepting female students under the same criteria for which they were accepting men. There was no bias against women. But at that time, few students were women because women were not applying to medical school (Cole, 1986). Thus, women acting under the assumption that medical schools are biased against women is an example of a self-sabotaging behavior.

Rebecca Pianta interviewed eleven female superintendents of several school districts in Southern California as part of her PhD dissertation work. Rebecca aimed to learn the self-sabotaging behaviors that limited the women as they rose to the top in the education field. Even though 75 percent of teachers are women in the United States, superintendent positions are the most male-dominated of any profession.

To be sure, several external factors contribute to the reduced number of women in the superintendent position. These challenges are similar to those faced in the corporate world, such as dealing with the good ole boys' network, unconscious bias, and sexist bosses. Still, it's even harder to face these barriers when engaging in self-sabotage.

**INSTEAD OF THINKING TOO SMALL, RECOGNIZE YOUR UNIQUE DESTINY**

Pianta explains that our patriarchal society has caused us to internalize typical stereotypes of women, which in turn causes us to miss out on our significant potential. We stay within our comfort zone. One difference between men and women is that men go for positions that allow them to take risks. Women will often disqualify themselves from a better situation if the job requires them to do something that they've never done before. If a man were asked, "How will you pull off this new project?" a man would guess the answer. In contrast, a woman would confess she had never pursued such a project before and disqualify herself from the assignment or the opportunity.

Soon after my mom was accepted into medical school, I took part in an exciting conversation with Peter, our next-door neighbor. He was a couple of years older than me, but we enjoyed talking, sometimes for hours. Peter had heard this riddle and was very interested in seeing how I would solve it. He introduced the story by saying, "A parent and son are in a car accident. The parent dies instantly, and the injured son is taken to the nearest hospital." Peter then shared, "The surgeon comes in and exclaims, 'I can't operate on this boy.'" Peter had an important lesson to teach me. Ends up, the surgeon was the son's mother. In my head, I had pictured the physician being the father.

Today, 48 percent of the students in medical school are female; however, when my mother applied, just under 30 percent were women. Mom's class had one hundred total students, and roughly ten of them were women (AAMC, 2014). Again, it wasn't that the women were not being accepted, it was about women not believing they would be allowed in and that lack of belief causing their enrollment to be lower than the men (Cole, 1986).

Pianta found that women who thought too small tended to minimize their value and made perfection their standard; therefore, they were not open to new experiences. Mom could have internalized her expected role and earned a doctorate in nursing. Mom also could have said, "I'm not the perfect candidate for medical school: older, married, with children and financial obligations." Instead, she didn't think small and didn't place undue perfectionistic standards on herself. She went for it and was rewarded for trying.

## INSTEAD OF FEAR AND WORRY, THINK ABOUT CONSTRUCTIVE PREPARATION

My daughter was born with giant congenital nevus, which means she has several large birthmarks all over her body. We affectionately call them dots, and they are located on her arms and legs. Our home is in the upper United States and our backyard faces a river wide enough for boating. She loves waving at the boats as they float by. Our favorite boat is the *Party Boat*, a vessel that hosts dinner parties with plenty of room for people to hang out near the side railings. Our daughter, from the start, loved waving at the people as they enjoyed their boat ride. She first encountered the boat in the spring when the temperature was cool enough to cover her arms and legs.

Upon the first summer day, with the temperature warm enough to wear shorts, she stopped waving at the people on the boats.

I asked her, "What is stopping you from gesturing to the boats?"

She said, "Because I don't want them to see my dots." My daughter perceived her dots as imperfections, and she believed the people on the boats would as well.

"If you let your dots stop you, what else will stop you in life?" I countered. She dropped everything and ran into the house. She was in shorts and a short-sleeved T-shirt when she returned, ready to greet the boat. My daughter let go of her fears.

So often, we can let fear and worry stop us from getting to the next level. Pianta describes the fear and worry as "a reaction to the discomfort of change" (Pianta, 2020). I define them as a belief in a forecasted failure. The problem is that you can use a forecasted failure to sabotage you from even starting a positive action or not attempting or not putting your best effort into a project.

You can use fear to assist you in listing all the reasons why a goal shouldn't be attempted. Alternatively, fear can be used to develop a constructive plan.

As far as applying to schools at an older age, Mom did her homework. She found a medical school that wanted to produce a different type of physician. They were looking for older students with diverse experiences. Rather than ignore or run from the potential problems, Mom prepared a plan to solve them before they became an issue.

### INSTEAD OF HOLDING BACK, ACT WITH CONFIDENCE

Pianta found holding back was women's second most self-sabotaging behavior. Some women worry that honestly expressing themselves will lead to others negatively evaluating them. This could hold true precisely when they are sharing a success or suggesting ways that things can be improved. These women fear that people will think they're egotistical and reject them if they share their achievements and ideas.

You're on a slippery slope if this is you, and it starts with not sharing your achievements and ideas. You will likely be overlooked when it comes to promotions and new challenges because no one knows about your successes and innovative thoughts. Following that, you'll become irritated when your value is not acknowledged. You can't win because you're operating in a catch-22 situation: If you talk about your accomplishments and inspirations, you will be shunned, and if you don't, you will be passed over. Once again, for emphasis, there is no way to win.

To progress, women need to show self-confidence by sharing their successes and solutions to problems. We need to authentically take credit for our contributions, whether they are in the past or future.

It could be difficult to identify and then share achievements. I know this feeling all too well. I was lucky enough to learn how to play the cello, the most beautiful-sounding stringed instrument in the orchestra. I played the cello in high school and earned a scholarship for college. I developed perfectionist tendencies in my cello playing. As a perfectionist, I could let one minor mistake ruin my impression of the whole performance. I would dwell on the one mistake, and when a person, visibly moved by the music, thanked me, I could hardly accept the praise. I was tempted to tell them how horrible the recital was. This was a mistake and Samantha had a better solution.

Samantha, a project manager, posted her story on LinkedIn about becoming a certified project manager during the COVID-19 lock-down period. Samantha shared:

"Obtaining my PMP in April 2021 after months of studying, with a newborn and nine-year-old schooling remotely during the pandemic, is one of the toughest things I have ever done. I scheduled my exam during my maternity leave…a week after giving birth… The odds were stacked against me as a tired and nursing mother, but I immersed myself in everything project management. YouTube videos, mobile applications that I studied…daily internet research, ordering as many books as possible, and a slew of mock tests. I was uncomfortable, tired, and nervous, but I did it! I took my exam with my baby and nine-year-old in the next room."

Samantha went on to say, "This post isn't to brag; this post is simply to say it is possible. Do not give up! I am a Project Manager with real, on-the-job experience and certification. I am proud!" (Downing, 2021).

Samantha found a way to present her hard work tastefully. She has tons of reasons to be proud of herself and be confident because her persistence and hard work paid off. Sam teaches us to not be afraid to shine our light because it's inspiring!

**INSTEAD OF DOING EVERYTHING YOURSELF, BUILD A POWER WEB**

Women, according to Pianta, often rely on themselves to learn new things instead of asking others for advice. In addition, when top female leaders reached out, they felt guilty for being an inconvenience. Among the most significant self-imposed obstacles women face are not enlarging their networks and then trying to do everything for themselves.

The fact is that women are rarely found in upper management functions, making it difficult or unnerving for them to establish extensive networks essential for advancement. Consequently, connecting with people outside of their network can be uncomfortable, and it will also seem to eat into precious time. Building beneficial relationships can be especially problematic when networking activities occur after regular working hours.

Regardless, it's important to talk with others, as difficult as it may seem, if only to explore what else is out there, as Shannon's story shows.

Shannon evolved her career starting from a computer programmer who developed business intelligence systems. However, she wanted more and decided to transition her career into project management. To make the transition, Shannon took on a temporary program manager role, and with that, she was able to work her way into becoming a senior project manager.

Prior to making her transition from programmer to a temporary project manager, it was vital to dialog with people occupying the role she was interested in. Shannon shares, "It was essential to talk with others—project managers, leaders, mentors, and sponsors—to quickly validate if product management was something for me."

Shannon could have prescribed to the idea that she must learn on her own. In that case, she would have applied for positions, not understood the gaps she needed to close, then not gotten the job and told herself, "I guess it's not in the cards for me to become a project manager." Instead, Shannon was smart. From her network, Shannon learned what skills she needed to "identify" in order to "close critical skill gaps." Shannon shows the importance of networking as it helped her transition her career to something she loved (Shi, 2021).

**INSTEAD OF GIVING AND RESENTING, GIVE AND SET BOUNDARIES**

Women often give, even when they don't want to, out of fear of saying no. When they do not wish to share but don't speak up to say so, or are more pleasant than they would like, they might end up feeling resentful. This sort of inauthentic giving, without healthy boundaries, leads to women being manipulated. The resentment can distract women from their career goals and becoming their best selves. Or it could leave them so busy, they do not have time to develop themselves powerfully. The result is burnout.

Women acting based on fear of conflict, judgment, and rejection is more common than men. Rather than putting ourselves first, we instead juggle multiple balls at once, distributing our attention among our jobs, career goals, family, and friends' needs. Instead of having a difficult conversation about what we need, we prefer to put our physical or mental health at risk rather than saying no.

Angela reports, "I speak from personal experience. My job as a vice president in a multi-billion-dollar organization was demanding. I oversaw large, global teams across multiple time zones and continents. In fact, I traveled so much that my own dog knew his dog sitter better than me. Because of my high ambitions set for the organization, I was willing to make personal sacrifices to ensure its success.

"In the wake of an organizational restructuring exercise, the expectation for our functional area had to be transformed while cutting costs and resources. Although I was nearly burnt out, I was so committed to the well-being of my team that I started pushing back more on their behalf than on my own. Finally, we were summoned to a team meeting that was scheduled in Europe over Memorial Day weekend. My direct reports had already made plans for family gatherings and barbecues and asked, 'Are you serious?' I let my manager know that asking the team to travel to that meeting would mean sacrificing the entire weekend with their families. The management team didn't understand, nor did they care. Eventually, we parted ways."

Angela offers this advice, "First, know that *reasonable* people will have a vested interest in accommodating a win/win solution, so be sensible and professional when stating your case and [offering] your manager options. Tell others what is in it for them as you set boundaries. Second, let go of those fears of judgment, conflict, and rejection and imagine how great you will feel when you speak up for yourself. Third, get buy-in from your manager in regard to the implementation and re-enforcement of the newly set boundaries." You will feel free when the boundaries are put into place (Meyburg, 2021).

**TAKING TIME TO SELF-REFLECT**
While Mom was working hard, she took time to step off the constantly moving hamster wheel long enough to self-reflect on her life, where she was, and where she wanted to go. When she contemplated her life, she dreamed big and acted on it. She thought about all the obstacles she might run into and, rather than letting problems stop her, she used that critical thinking to proactively navigate around issues. When she got stuck, she reached out to others for help. She also set boundaries, sharing with others, including us kids, what it

was that she needed to succeed. Through taking these steps, she was able to begin her journey.

Scan the QR code to access bonus items.

**CHAPTER 3**

# Creating a Positive Vision

—

"Once you awaken your inner genius, you will find your true identity and purpose."

"Doctors leave caring for the patient to us nurses. Their bedside manner is poor, and they rely on us to clean up the emotional mess they leave behind. Taking an interest in patients is an important part of their job. There is no doubt that doctors should be as attentive to each patient as we are," I overheard my mom complain to Aunt Michelle. "When I become a doctor, my focus will be on paying attention to what the patient says and being kind—along with knowing medicine. I believe in doing so, I will holistically keep my patients healthy."

Mom had a motivational vision and mission depicting the type of physician she wanted to become. Mom didn't just have a goal of becoming a physician; she had a dream. Her plans were clear to her: she saw how she wanted to present herself and knew how she wanted to be perceived. She had radiant energy of kindness, intelligence, and certainty about her. She would tell you her goal was to survive during medical school, but from my perspective, she was on a mission because she had a vision.

It ends up that having a mission is very essential to your success: "Mission-driven workers are 54 percent more likely to stay for five years at a company and 30 percent more likely to grow into high performers than those who arrive at work with only their paycheck as the motivator" (Ross, 2015). We are emotional creatures, and a motivating vision gives us the why for belonging to an organization.

Researchers have identified two types of personal visions: a positive emotion attractor (PEA) vision and a negative emotion attractor (NEA) vision (Boyatzis, 2015). Both concepts involve emotions, hormones, and neurons; however, the emotions, hormones, and neurons utilized differ. Both processes are valuable in shattering barriers. That said, what matters most, and the key, is when and how often we use either one of them.

I define the positive emotion attractor (PEA) as a motivating mental picture of what could be that inspires you to act and reach beyond your current state of being. This method asks us to picture ourselves as our highest or best self. In other words, we work toward a purpose.

Capturing a vision is as simple as daydreaming and becoming excited about a potential future. It ends up that there is a physiological event that happens when we catch that glimpse of what it is we should be about. When we experience that positive emotional energy, we engage the vagus nerve. The vagus nerve is a particular neural pathway connecting our brain and heart.

Our values, actions, and passions line up when we engage the vagus nerve. Our work seems to flow when our hearts and minds are aligned. We are doing something we are passionate about and contributing to our best future. Like my mom, those who can activate the vagus nerve are on a mission because of their vision.

To exercise the vagus nerve, we relax and dream about our best selves—without evaluating those dreams. We open ourselves to new ideas and an improved life, without judgment.

Additionally, we engage emotions such as hope, joy, and fun, which causes the release of the hormone called oxytocin. The combined effect of the vagus nerve and oxytocin leads you to engage in the learning process that propels you to something new (Boyatzis, 2015).

The negative emotion attractor (NEA) visioning involves neurons related to paying greater attention to detail. Additionally, the NEA releases hormones called epinephrine and norepinephrine. The combined effect of the TPN-based neurons and epinephrine hormones triggers a person to pay attention to detail. Unfortunately, the NEA system also shuts off the creative thinking process (Boyatzis, 2015).

Both systems are helpful, but it's physiologically impossible to activate both methods simultaneously. When the PEA system is on and you dream, the NEA, paying attention to detail, is turned off. Likewise, when paying attention to detail, the dreaming system is turned off.

The trick is learning how to oscillate between the two parts of your brain, the NEA and the PEA. In doing so, you will maximize your brain power.

Sofia is someone who actively thinks creatively and pays attention to detail. She knows how and when to activate her two brain parts. Sofia, the assistant controller working at a university in the United States, illustrates how to use the two visioning processes. Sofia was a tireless and hard worker who, midway into her career, decided it was time for her to move to the next level within her organization. She had just earned a master's degree in accounting and was working on obtaining a CPA license. Sofia had been in her current role for several years and wanted a new challenge. The vice president role opened, and she decided to throw her name in the hat.

Her team was well known for getting work done quietly and efficiently. She'd received accolades for coming up with innovative tools through which the university could save money, earning millions of dollars of savings. The university knew they could count on Sofia and her team to deliver on time and with high quality. The next rung in her career was, logically, to become vice president of the university's financial department. Her qualifications ticked most of the boxes when comparing her experience and skills to the job description.

Sofia passed the first round of interviews. Only four applicants would make it to the final round. A large committee would interview the final candidates in a big conference room before meeting with the organization's top leader. Ultimately, Sofia did not get the promotion.

After really thinking about not being selected, Sofia decided to have a deep conversation with herself. As she went through the interview process, she had to admit to herself that a part of her didn't feel excited about getting the job. An essential part of her felt drawn to teaching.

She daydreamed about using her vast experiences and CPA credential to teach undergraduate students. She envisioned the type of lessons she would lead in the college environment. Sofia could see herself enjoying teaching well into her eighties. She also linked her imagined future with how she would spend her time personally on the side.

When Sofia didn't get the promotion, she was in part relieved because it now meant she could pursue her teaching dream. When she relaxed and exercised her vagus nerve, a fire of passion rose in her heart—one that never came alive while she was undergoing the interview process. She engaged her vagus nerve and had a different vision and mission that she now intended to go after.

Sofia's first vision to be her department's vice president was born from what she thought she should be or do since it was the natural next step on the ladder. This vision was based upon the negative emotion attractor system. The image that filled her daydreams, on the other hand, was Sofia's positive emotion attractor dream.

When we envision our future from the NEA perspective, we will feel frustrated and betrayed over time for pursuing a dream we were not passionate about. Therefore, it is imperative to determine your next career step by first engaging the PEA.

I met Evelyn when she was working in the marketing department of a major diagnostic company. Her role was to create technical documents describing the science behind diagnostic tests. Diagnostic test results are an essential part of medicine: the results provide physicians with the information they need to prescribe the therapies patients require. Eventually, Evelyn's career evolved.

While Evelyn started out by creating the technical marketing materials for one department, over time all clinical areas came to report to her, including infectious disease, cardiovascular medicine, and cancer. In her words, leading the entire department "was great fun. It was challenging. They recruited me because I had a strong scientific background and led one of the fastest-growing clinical areas. They came to me and asked if I would like to lead this team."

Evelyn was a well-respected and successful executive—and she was also majorly stressed, and her health was suffering. She gained unwanted weight, and the stress severely disrupted her sleep. Meanwhile, percolating in Evelyn's imagination was a dream of owning a business. She wanted to help other people, particularly other women, with their businesses while also helping with their health. She tried to make a difference in other people's lives in her own business instead of doing something for somebody else. Evelyn was frustrated about not pursuing the dream she envisioned in her head and heart.

Eventually, Evelyn found a way to own a business helping others achieve success while staying healthy. In her words, "I sometimes think it was divine intervention. God knew I was majorly stressed, and it wasn't good for my health, and I wasn't doing the things that needed to be done, so he created a big change for me. I see ladies from my corporate days; they say I'm a different person, healthy now. I lost twenty-five pounds, and I fall asleep when my head hits the pillow. That didn't happen before."

Evelyn explained, "It's interesting to know that people see that transformation. In the corporate world, I was so driven. I'm driven now in my coaching business, and that's why I'm successful with my business. The difference is that I love sharing more about my story. I love being able to help people now on a different level and helping women who feel stuck themselves. Today, it is amazing to see how I can help others make changes. I help people with so many things such as losing weight, gaining a new career, a new perspective, making changes toward better mental health, increasing financial freedom, and so many different things." Evelyn pursued a vision developed through positive emotions and enjoys the future it generated for her.

Imagination and passion matter. It's essential first to imagine and be passionate about a fantastic future before devising a path to make that future happen. Knowing the precise way to become your best self is not essential at first because the approach reveals itself over time.

While working as a sales director at a top diagnostic company, the same company as Evelyn, I noticed we were not onboarding sales reps smoothly and effectively. Poor onboarding meant new members of the sales team took longer to close deals because they didn't know the company products as well as they should or could have.

To become a successful sales executive, you must be competent. If a sales representative doesn't know their products thoroughly, their customers will not value nor trust them. Those who are the most successful in sales are respected and trusted by their clients.

As the Director of Sales, my role was to manage my team to generate revenue growth on a specific timetable. I anticipated a standard ramp-up period of learning for the new sales representatives I brought into the company. The problem was that my new hires were not ramping up as quickly and as well as they needed because training was lacking.

I checked in with my colleagues and learned they were experiencing the same problem. When we compared our notes, we discovered the training program wasn't working. I knew we could do better. I thought about the type of program we could institute and outlined my thoughts to the vice president of sales.

I presented the problem and showed him the general outline of how we could initiate a blended learning training program that would be more effective for all teams. I envisioned a program that allowed new sales hires to access materials via the internet using online videos and podcasts rather than in the classroom alone. I also thought about ways we could track progress and provided a general capstone assignment at the end of training.

My goal in presenting the idea was to gain the vice president of sales input because I wanted to submit the concept to the current director of training. My intention was to assist in putting the program together if the organization was interested. My passion was powered by a drive to develop others and grow the business. I thought my approach would mature the sales team faster, thereby helping us produce more business quickly. I imagined a better future for the organization and the new hires.

I didn't know how to execute my plan, meaning the specific know-how needed to put together learning videos and import them into a management system. I also didn't know that the current director of training had turned in his resignation. He wanted to retire. The following week, the vice president of sales offered me the director position. I executed my plan of training the entire sales team of two hundred individuals because of my vision and mission of growing people.

As I shared earlier, the two types of visions—PEA and NEA—are not turned on at the same time because each pathway stops the other from working (Heaphy and Dutton, 2008). The inspirational neural pathway needs to be activated first.

Following inspiration, you can use the NEA to discover how to make the vision happen.

As I said before, I did not know precisely how to execute the sales training plan; however, I knew I could figure it out using the NEA neurons. In other words, I could figure out how to implement the project using critical thinking. Many training programs employ a blended system, meaning courses are taught through video, podcasts, and classrooms. I just had to reverse engineer the process. Additionally, my team and I needed to review the learning objectives, identify missing content, and decide the best medium via which to teach the lessons. By engaging the NEA at the right time, we created a great training program.

Had I engaged the NEA from the very beginning, I would never have come up with the idea of a blended learning system. My NEA neurons would have told me, "Hey, this isn't your problem; leave it alone." Instead, I listened to my PEA neurons, and they said to me, "Hey, wouldn't it be great if we could create this effective training program?"

With dreaming, timing comes first. Imagining a better future must happen without the NEA network during the positive dream stage because the NEA will shut the whole process down. Likewise, it's important not to engage other people's NEA during the dreaming process. It would be best if you first paint the picture that you love. Keep the PEA in play until you see the complete image it is delivering to you.

You can feel when a person is on a mission because she is excited about what she is about to do. Take, for example, Kim

Ng. Kim is the first female general manager for the Marlins, a men's major league baseball team. Kim also is a winner of the Forbes 50 Over 50 award.

In the video presented on the Forbes website, Kim explains the need for a dream. Her dream gave her the strength of perseverance. It took ten interviews and nine rejections before she landed her dream job as general manager. Kim speaks of the importance of starting with a PEA-inspired vision (which, again, comes from the heart). She explains the importance of knowing yourself, which she next ascertained through activating her NEA at the right time.

She shares that it's important to self-reflect and understand what is most important to you (via the PEA system). You can fully detail your "why" to others. Others knowing your "why" helps them to promote you in your cause (Forbes, 2021).

"Visioning is a process of putting into words a future that one wishes to create" (Amuah, 2012) and has special meaning for you. Your vision is one you are excited about, know is achievable, and allows you to grow and stretch yourself in the process. A grand vision causes your palms to sweat as you think about some of the steps you'll need to execute to achieve it. A mission is the purpose of the dream. The mission defines the results that will happen because you implemented the idea.

My vision for revamping sales training was to create an engaging program while ramping the sales team up faster. I wanted to ensure that they knew our product inside out and understood how customers would benefit from it. I felt the modules had to be engaging and to the point. In executing this vision, I felt those who joined our team would quickly ramp up their business and be successful in the long term. The sales representatives' achievements would lead to success for our company.

My mother's vision was to become a caring physician who took time to listen to her patients so that she could treat them holistically. Her mission was to ensure her patients were healthy and happy individuals. Now that Mom had activated her PEA system, it was time for her to use the other part of her brain to determine how she would achieve success. Mom needed to break the cycle to transition her life from being a nurse to being a physician.

Scan the QR code to access a meditation to activate your unique vision.

**CHAPTER 4**

# Breaking the Cycle

---

"Embrace the unique gifts you offer the world."

In my teenage mind, I took it as a matter of fact: *Don't all moms apply to medical school?* I didn't realize her path was unique until I was much older. My career ups and downs helped me appreciate my mother's journey to becoming a health care provider. I asked, "Mom, what made you decide to attend medical school?"

"Well, Natalie," I could see mom looking inward at her memories, "remember the delicatessen we owned in Oak Forest, Illinois?"

My mind immediately went back to that deli. I both loved and hated it. My parents opened their first store and called it "Country Deli." It started as a small retail location, offering lunch meats and cheeses, spices, sauces, and delicious sandwiches. Later, Mom and Dad expanded Country Deli to also sell liquor.

It was a family-owned business down to the core. Dad built the shelves from scratch, and we kids stocked them. The moment I was tall enough to reach the counter with the help of a stepping stool, I was at the cash register ringing up customers. Our clients were amazed that a ten-year-old could count out their change as well as any adult. It made me proud!

While it was rewarding to learn new skills working at the stores, I hated the stores because I felt they robbed me and my siblings of our childhood fun. When other kids were playing baseball across the street, our whole family loaded into the car and headed to work at the store. I was jealous of my neighborhood friends' free spirits. We three kids had responsibilities to attend to; there was no room for playing.

"Well," Mom explained now, decades after leaving the deli in our past, "one slow day, we had no customers, and I was sitting on the stool in the back next to the sink and daydreaming when the idea struck me: I should become a physician. And that was that."

Surprised, I expected more. "Really, Mom? Just like that, and that was all?"

"I guess I asked myself why I shouldn't become a physician."

"And?" I queried, thinking of a whole long list of arguments she could have generated.

"I couldn't come up with one reason I couldn't overcome… So, yes, that was it. There wasn't any reason I couldn't become a physician."

My adult brain silently generated a long list of obstacles to mom becoming a physician. Then I realized, she was right: we could overcome all the problems that would get in her way.

Mom also explained, "The way things were going with owning the stores wasn't ideal. I never saw your father because he was always working. I didn't enjoy being a nurse because the way physicians treated me. So, there was that as well."

What struck me about Mom's answer was that she had a way of daydreaming constructively. I realized my daydreaming time wasn't beneficial like hers. My mind tended to continuously replay what I perceived was going wrong rather than imagine ways to solve what bothered me. As I would mull over the adverse experiences, I felt trapped, like a victim, and I became depressed after thinking about them. This led me to believe I didn't have any good choices. I didn't feel my daydreaming was useful like my mother's.

Instead of focusing on feeling stuck with a store going bankrupt, becoming angry with the existing and challenging financial situation, or giving up and devolving into feeling complacent, Mom broke free. Mom gave herself room to fantasize, imagine what it would be like to live the dream, and believe she could make it a reality. Many women don't break free of the negative "victim complex, anger, complacency, victim complex again" cycle. Mom's path was to acknowledge the parts of her life that were working and those that were not. She envisioned a better future and made it happen by taking small steps toward her vision.

She didn't judge or blame herself or others for whatever adverse event disturbed her. Mom could have criticized Dad for opening the stores and the physicians for bellowing at her. Instead, she observed the condition, trusting in her understanding of the problem, and moved beyond the pain. Mom spent her time dreaming of a new possibility and then decided to move toward it. Furthermore, Mom listed the obstacles she would have to overcome to obtain her goal.

Other people, like Tomi, have also dreamed constructively.

Tomi, a media coordinator, had enough stress and constant anxiety at work. Tomi was done with being burned out and decided the best way out of the cycle was to take a "gap year" to learn more about herself and what she loved and didn't love doing in her career. She needed to create a plan to switch paths. Taking an interval of time away from stress seemed like the best path to navigate to a new track. Following her intuition, Tomi enrolled in a data and business analysis course during her gap year. This turned out to be an excellent move, since she learned that she loved it.

Within a year, Tomi secured a job as a senior executive data analyst. Tomi's experience perfectly points out the need for women to catch themselves in the negative cycle of feeling like a victim, getting angry, then complacent, and then a victim again. Tomi removed herself from the negative progression by slowing down, stepping away, and meditating daily. Others can step away by just sitting still or walking, and daydreaming of ways they can take themselves to a higher level (Ajumobi, 2021).

Paula, like Tomi, realized she needed to exit the negative progression toward burnout. Paula was a hard-charging business executive who decided to slow down. After sensing she was exhausted, she confirmed the source of the extreme fatigue by reviewing her travel logs. She had a pedal-to-the-metal type of energy, which led her to travel 85 percent of the time. Paula had felt overtired until then but hadn't analyzed her travel schedule. Once she reviewed her logs, she discovered just how much she was pushing it. The wise little voice in her head told her she would die in just a few months if she didn't slow down!

Paula realized the value of slowing down and checking in with herself. From her perspective, this new awareness was an awakening, learning to understand and deal with her high drive for results and listening to her intuition. Paula explains, "We live in that space, and it's very much…dog eat dog and…jungle out there… There's got to be a pain if you want the [gain] right? It was really just about being tough, working your ass off, and being in the grind. So many people live in that, but actually, it's a very depleting state." Paula decided she wanted more than balance alone because that would just be keeping the exhaustion at bay by seeking a little more stability. To get out of the negative cycle completely, she had to do more than just find a balance; she needed to step out of the loop. Paula took a retreat to India to activate her creative brain and discover what she wanted to do. Today, Paula is a coach, helping others slow down to trigger the creative part of their brain.

Mom, Tomi, and Paula all articulated for themselves the things that were not working and then identified a situation they would appreciate. They all felt it was essential to identify the goals they should go for, and they truly believed in themselves. They believed in their abilities and went for what was better for them, taking charge of their lives.

The decision to go for more takes you out of the cycle. In other words, you take control of your future and become self-efficacious. Being self-efficacious first involves feeling confident enough in your abilities to accomplish tasks and find solutions to problems. It also means setting goals for yourself and taking the steps needed to move forward to achieve those goals. To break free from the cycle of victim complex, anger, and complacency, you must accumulate positive experiences. These experiences give you the confidence to believe you can achieve a dream. If you don't have the experience, you'll need to lean on past related successful events and, potentially, coaches and mentors. You need to rely on faith—faith in your ability to learn, persevere, and find mentors and other resources—to guide you to your chosen path.

The first step my mom, Tomi, and Paula took to visualize their best selves was acknowledging where they were and what was not working for them anymore. These brave women accepted they were in a place that wasn't serving them. They all trusted the wisdom of their intuition and decided on a different future. They embraced an imaginative lot that would work for them and stepped into it, moving forward.

My mom broke free of the negative thought cycle as she sat daydreaming on a stool next to a sink. I don't make it a habit of sitting on stools; too uncomfortable! I don't know of anyone else with a similar practice. Still, I know that many inspirational leaders make it a daily routine to meditate. Intentionally meditate. In doing so, they take themselves to a higher level.

Gabby Bernstein, *New York Times* best-selling author of nine books, international speaker, and spiritual coach, is one of my all-time favorite go-to sources of insights. I've purchased her "Transform Fear to Faith" digital course and find it a great source of inspiration. At the end of the first presentation, Gabby was asked to list her number one daily habit that has transformed her life. "Meditation," Gabby answered. She went on to say, "The one habit that most successful people do that you probably would admire is to meditate. The one habit that people you feel connected to when you witness them or feel a sense of authenticity is that they're likely a meditator. It's just shedding all of the stories and beliefs that we've placed upon ourselves to come back to the truth of who we are. And it's a mental shower that clears you. And it sounds so cliche, but it's the truth. It's the answer."

Admittedly, my meditation practice is in its infancy. Thankfully, there are many ways to listen to our still, small voice. Others have found that walking, running, and biking are also meditative. Some people have discovered journaling facilitates connecting to their intuition. Whatever works best for you, you'll need to slow down and give yourself permission to dream big.

Sara worked in several organizations that cared for the elderly, be it a house call physician practice, a hospital, or a busy nursing home. Sara was passionate about what she did and poured her soul into her work. Wherever Sara was employed, she always became the "go-to" person at every location she was retained because of her work ethic. She wasn't interested in becoming the CEO of an existing company. However, she was intelligent and driven enough to do so. Instead, Sara had a heart for delivering value. But working her way up the ladder would mean spending time on activities that were not important to her.

While working for an employer, Sara strove to deliver value. She had a clear vision of the impact she wanted to provide organizations. Additionally, she discovered she wanted to serve the elderly in the nursing home. It wasn't until she overcame breast cancer that she moved her dream to the next level. She soon realized she wanted to provide value to nursing homes in a way that other consultant companies were not. She wanted to try to do so at an affordable price. Today, Sara is a consultant and the CEO of her own thriving business. Her vision and passion have caused her to be a sought-after expert in elder care. More importantly, Sara loves what she does because it was born out of her heart-driven vision.

If you could do anything, and I were to tell you it's possible, what would you love to do? What impact would you want to make? It's time to have faith in yourself, your voice, and your inner guide. Things will not always go according to plan. But by taking one logical step every day, you will be able to feel confident and achieve your goals. There's no sense in feeling like you have to be an expert or do it all by yourself to get started. You can gather mentors around you or take classes to achieve your dreams. There is no time like now.

You don't have to wait for everything in your life to be perfect to get started. All you need to do is take the first faith-filled step forward.

Access bonus items such as pictures, a guided meditation, music lists, and other goodies through the QR code.

**CHAPTER 5**

# Step Forward and Keep Moving

---

*"Dreams that matter never die, but every now and again, they just need a little more fuel."*

Once Mom decided to become a kind and holistic healthcare provider, she took three decisive and distinct steps and then kept moving forward. "Mom," I asked. "How did you know what to do to get into the DO school? Did you have a university counselor to tell you what to do?"

"No mentors of any sort, no previous women to tell me what they did, and it wasn't easy. In retrospect, it was hard. I left my family and friends to achieve this new reality," she recalled.

The question was: How did Mom keep moving forward with this dream without her daily grind killing it? The excitement of a vision can be quickly extinguished in the light of real-life pressures. In my mom's case, the idea stuck. How did she keep moving forward to the point that her vision overcame the everyday stresses of life and the fear of leaving family and friends behind?

"So, how did you know what moves to make?" I pressed again, considering the questions in the back of my mind.

"I took one step forward, then two, then three—one step at a time," Mom answered.

"What was your first action item on the list?" I asked.

"My first move was to clear out the old before welcoming in the new," Mom responded in her wise voice.

The first step that became physically visible to me was Mom creating a space dedicated to filling out medical school applications. Our old filing cabinets were shoved into the garage and replaced with a new table in her home office to organize her thoughts, information, and school papers. "You kids," I recall her setting down the rules, "are not to touch this table." I admired the carefully stacked piles of paper. Mom gathered references, certificates, and other correspondence needed for her applications. She had to stay organized because she applied to thirteen schools over two years.

Beyond that, energetically and emotionally, Mom needed to stretch and strengthen her self-belief to imagine herself as a physician. It was a demonstratively different place for her. I remember Mom coming home and complaining to Dad about how physicians treated other nurses at the hospital.

Unlike the majority of physicians she had met so far, she would speak to all people respectfully, regardless of their level of education.

I can relate to the validity of clearing out an old self-image to replace it with a reimagined one. I had to view myself in a new light when I was accepted into graduate school as a PhD candidate for molecular biology, cell biology, biochemistry, and biophysics. While I had received lots of feedback that I was intellectually sharp, I didn't feel smart. When comparing myself to others I, in fact, thought it took me a lot of time to understand concepts. I sometimes allowed other people's opinions to override mine at work when internally I felt we were going in the wrong direction. I didn't speak up. Instead, I was quiet.

My admittance to graduate school meant I would become an authority in some area of science. Being accepted to graduate school gave me the proof I needed to finally stop discounting my own thoughts and opinions.

Likewise, before moving to a new position or environment, we need to clear out the old negative energy to make room for the higher positive force. It's necessary to understand what thoughts and behaviors may have contributed to poor outcomes in the past. If we don't clear out the old, negative thoughts, we will bring toxic environments, bullies, and negative situations with us. It is as if the old world will haunt us like ghostly spirits. The adverse situation we attempted to escape will appear in the new environment. Through a willingness to bravely understand our part in a negative case, we can transition to letting go, going big, rising, and stepping into our power. We bring forth our own greatness through this commitment to understanding and growing ourselves. We must first clear out the old before the new enters our lives.

After unblocking a space for the new, Mom completed her homework. She knew exactly the type of physician she wanted to be and took the time to research various schools she was applying to. She tried to find a match between the two. Mom's goal was to enter a school that produced physicians aligned with her values. Thus, she sought to understand the type of physician each school strived to create. The reward of the research was that the school she was ultimately accepted into synced up perfectly with her values. Mom was accepted into the Kansas City University College of Osteopathic Medicine. The school wanted to train its students to be caring and compassionate physicians. It valued diversity, including experiences, race, age, and gender. Consequently, older students were boldly accepted. She found a home.

Mom's final step in faithfully moving forward was simply believing in herself. She came up with a list of reasons to be confident. She recorded the positive experiences she garnered both as a nurse and a businesswoman running the stores, as each bit of praise helped lead to success. Teachers had showered Mom with compliments when she solved complex diagnostic cases. Mom soon learned she was an excellent convergent thinker. She also worked with other naturally talented women, though they had doctorates in nursing. She found shining examples and role models in laboring with these brilliant women. She also gained confidence by trying and failing. Mom made mistakes, and her mentors were there to patiently help her learn from her blunders. Mom was treated with respect during both good times and bad. There were essential people supporting her through thick and thin.

Research shows that self-belief, or self-efficacy, is a trait all leaders use to get ahead. Those with self-belief will view their experiences positively, knowing that each learning opportunity is a chance to grow. Women with self-belief see that they don't have to be 100 percent proficient the first time they attempt something new. Instead, they are taught through a process of learning from failure. Thus, when undertaking new projects, they stay patient with themselves. These women release unfair expectations of perfection when attempting unfamiliar and challenging assignments.

Personally, I've struggled with imposing unfair expectations of success on myself when learning new skills in playing tennis. For example, I sometimes get frustrated with my hitting during lessons. During one tennis lesson, my impatience became apparent when I struggled to hit volleys well in a challenging situation. I just wasn't getting the concept the coach was trying to convey and was missing what I told myself were easy volleys. Then, when I finally "got it," instead of celebrating a new skill, I criticized myself for taking so long to get it right.

As I viewed the situation from outside myself, I realized it was my coach's job to put me in challenging situations so that I could learn and grow. I needed to exert more self-compassion as I worked toward confronting more complex situations. Likewise, I celebrate when I am successful. I also discovered the importance of taking stock of my self-judgment. I found a self-block: I needed to relax when in new and taxing conditions. Learning would likely occur faster when I reduced my anxiety. Also, tennis lessons would be much more enjoyable if I weren't so hard on myself. I would have never discovered the block if I wasn't putting myself in a perplexing position. Now that I can anticipate my tendency and triggers, I can catch myself and nip self-criticism before it gets out of hand!

The key to Mom's ability to take action on her vision was to believe in herself, be patient while learning, and surround herself with supportive people.

In addition to feeling confident, Mom needed to speak positively about herself. To speak in a self-assured manner, Mom needed a list of the competencies the medical school leaders felt were necessary for success. Competency is defined as the ability to use skills and knowledge to perform an important job. Take, for example, conflict management. Conflict management is the knack for creating cooperative relationships even when people disagree. Those unskilled in this may avoid situations of disagreement and give up too soon when people are upset. Those who overuse conflict management skills may get in the middle of everyone else's problems.

Mom needed to tie the skills the school required with her self-believed talents. This was when Mom engaged the analytical part of her brain.

Like Mom, after generating a vision with the creative side of your brain, it's time for you to use the other part. The analytical portion of your brain will help you decipher the next steps in moving forward and articulate to others why you and why now. You can use this part of your brain to generate a plan by asking questions about what it takes to be successful, the skills needed, and the experience required. These are natural and essential questions.

It takes experience to move into a different position. Yet, sometimes, you can't gain new experience unless you have existing on-the-job training. It's a chicken and egg problem. Which comes first? To solve the glitch, you'll need to identify transferable skills. A transferable skill is a quality you can take from one role to another. Communication, organization, dependability, and conflict management are transferable skills. Identifying the traits required for the position you desire and showing how you've illustrated those skills will help you overcome the "which comes first" problem.

Your action plan begins with carefully acquiring a list of competencies required for success, networking effectively, and skillfully promoting yourself.

Sulaf earned a bachelor's degree in computer science and was gainfully employed as a teacher when war broke out in her country of Iraq. She and her family fled to Jordan along with thousands of others. The conflict lasted longer than expected. Soon, it became evident that Sulaf had to seek employment in the new country. By then, millions of people had fled like Sulaf. In fact, it was estimated that about 1.8 million people were displaced from Iraq to neighboring countries at that time. Sulaf had to find a way to stand out among all the other job seekers because there were far more applicants than jobs available.

While Sulaf could find a job teaching computer skills, she found the role boring and wanted to widen her skillset. She had stretched herself to learn more and took a free course about managing stocks. She then became inspired to teach others about the stock market. Sulaf described how she could transfer her teaching skills to instruct others on how to manage stocks and bonds. She was able to find employment with a multinational company, which then eventually relocated her to America. Despite the crowded job market and no direct experience teaching others how to manage stocks, Sulaf successfully navigated her career to another teaching topic by stressing transferable skills.

As Sulaf described, "The end result is I have more confidence. I know that I can recreate myself if I ever need to change again. Once you've done it a few times, you become more sure of yourself."

Mom faithfully took action by first clearing unproductive, disempowering thoughts. In doing so, she created a space for a new, more powerful self-image. She then took stock of her values and identified possible medical schools that aligned with her dream. Mom then developed reasons for self-belief by creating a list of explanations for why she should feel confident. From there, she developed a catalog of competencies she would later transfer to her career as a physician. Her next steps were to fully articulate why she should be admitted to medical school on her application. In other words, she had to learn how to brag about herself.

Access bonus items such as pictures, a guided meditation, music lists, and other goodies through the QR code.

## CHAPTER 6

# Stand Up and Brag!

---

*"A positive presence attracts positive responses."*

As she stood at the front door with the freshly sealed and stamped envelopes in her hand, butterflies danced inside of her: she couldn't predict what would happen next. She was putting herself out there, taking the risk of being rejected. "It's going to be okay," Mom whispered to herself as she carefully placed the envelopes in the mailbox.

Raising the flag so that the postal service would swiftly deliver the applications to their prospective sites, she thought, *It's done. There is no turning back. We are doing this.*

Mom sent off thirteen applications that day, resulting in two interviews. She knew that medical schools were looking for students who possessed essential competencies to ensure that they would become capable healthcare providers. Some of these competencies included being service-oriented, having social skills, teamworking, and resilience (AAMC, 2022). Mom needed to know the list of competencies the medical school was interested in. She also needed to identify examples of how she embodied these traits for conversing with the schools' admission boards.

In order to be accepted into medical school, Mom had to articulate her strengths and then present them in a manner that would resonate with those who interviewed her. Additionally, talking about her skills had to feel natural to her. Mom's responses to questions had to illustrate that she possessed the competencies they were interested in. Since Mom was a businesswoman and a nurse, she had a natural ability to illustrate the benefits of her experiences.

For example, Mom didn't shy away from complicated projects. Instead, she used these projects to grow her leadership skills, such as helping the university start a daycare to planning graduation ceremonies. Mom embraced demanding tasks and then proudly spoke about the work she did. The results of those projects were used to illustrate her leadership skills. She knew how to promote herself.

Like Mom, it's essential you understand the competencies needed for success and then link skills with the new position you are going after. However, women generally feel that speaking positively about what they accomplished means bragging. Unfortunately, by bragging, women believe they are bringing unnecessary attention to themselves (Carlin, 2018; Buse, 2014). They are not.

I can relate to having a difficult time bragging about my success; however, I found it was necessary to get over my resistance. I once had transitioned to a new boss that wasn't very fond of me, didn't understand me, and didn't believe in my sales talent. While as a sales professional, I consistently produced growth year after year, he disagreed with my style.

I didn't prescribe to the notion that to produce sales, you had to see a vast number of people. I believed you had to be innovative and understand your clients, in particular the problems they were facing, and provide the right solutions to the right people. I took time to get to know my customer base, focusing on their issues and projects, then kept meticulous notes of all I learned about them. Using this knowledge of my clients, I approached them with tailored solutions. My clients loved me for getting to know them so well.

My approach was very different from my new boss's process. He thought I didn't work hard enough because I didn't ascribe to the "numbers game." Playing the numbers game meant that in order to hit your sales goals, you needed to talk to tons of people. I believed, instead, you didn't need to talk to tons of people—you needed to talk to the right people at the right time. Because I wasn't talking to large numbers of people, like other sales representatives were, the new boss was skeptical about my ability to continue growing the business.

Despite the fact I hit my sales goals, I was worried about what he would say when review time came. Fortunately, the company let the employee fill out our review profiles before the boss completed his portion of the employee evaluation. I took the time to document my yearly results and the methods by which I achieved my goals. I clearly pointed out that I first focused on specific products and then created a three-pronged approach to determine the best promotional strategy. Once I identified the most productive method, I rolled the plan out to the rest of my district.

This proactive process of articulating my methods worked well, and I could tell I won my boss over because of his response to the questions. Initially, his evaluation of me was harsh; however, his opinions were glowing by the end of the report. Had I not confidently bragged about myself in the review document, my boss's review of me would have been poor.

You need to take on complex assignments that broaden and stretch you to advance your career. Once completed, you must speak proudly about the positive outcomes and results.

In early 2002, Sharifah, a thirty-year-old document officer in Malaysia, was asked to assist the company's engineering manager in a complex project. The organization needed Sharifah's help to erect its first building to facilitate its expanding R&D operations team. They started the project from scratch: from selecting the most suitable location to ensuring the infrastructure, utilities, and amenities were on spec and that the build was within budget.

The project was intense, and Sharifah had to concentrate on her document control job in the mornings. Right after lunch, she got to work on completing the extraordinary building venture. Her afternoons were spent making site visits, collecting all the relevant data, and compiling the information into comparison tables for the management to review.

Once the site was selected, Sharifah needed to work on the building's design and aesthetics. The look and feel of the building reflected the company's image, but the architect had a tough time pleasing the boss. Sharifah needed to keep the boss happy and motivate the architect to complete the job to the boss's liking. The timeline was aggressive—a four-month challenge—but Sharifah got it done.

Sharifah was relieved when the building was finalized because she could return to a regular full-time job instead of juggling her time between the project and her everyday work. In Sharifah's words, "It was then our engineering manager… offered me [the job of running] the facility."

When asked to run the facility, Sharifah recalls, "I actually immediately said no!"

The engineering manager asked her, "Why not?"

She replied, "I think it's beyond my capabilities, and I'm not qualified for it."

The engineering manager countered, "I've seen your work on the project. I believe you are the most capable and the best-suited person to do it. I know you love the building."

She discerned one factor in working with her company: "You'd always be pushed into the pool's deep end. It's up to you whether you will sink or float." She decided she would learn to swim.

Sharifah was lucky there was a leader in her organization that recognized her talents. Not everyone is so fortunate.

When taking the initiative to transition to another position, like Mom, you must discover the transferable skills and competencies to present in interview. You'll need to articulate your talent to others, sometimes strangers, in a way that resonates with them and also feels authentic and natural to you.

Hiring managers want interviews to go well; they want to be made aware of potential employees' gifts and talents and understand how they think. As a hiring business director, my goal was to find the best person for the job, which meant getting applicants to stand out during interviews. I encouraged candidates to overtly share inspirational stories like Sharifah's and the processes by which they achieved those results.

I not only wanted to validate that the results recorded on their résumé were accurate, but I also paid attention to how they shared their stories. I wanted to be aware of their thought processes.

Every person has encountered obstacles on the job. I was interested in understanding the complexity of the challenges the candidate had to overcome. The candidate needed to show me how they successfully navigated through difficult situations, at least as demanding, if not more so, than those they would encounter in the role I was interviewing for. I wanted to grasp how the candidates applied positive thinking and creativity to overcome demanding situations and reach their goals.

During interviews, I asked, "How did you achieve such remarkable results?" To my dismay, I found that candidates often described the actions of other team members instead of their part in the success of a project. There was no mention by the candidate of the steps they personally took to accomplish the results. It's nice to credit others; however, it did not provide the confidence in what their specific role was and left me with an impression that the candidate placed in another environment would fail.

I had hired Denise, and since then, my job focus changed, and she has moved on to other hiring managers. "I wonder, Denise," I inquired while catching up with her on a coffee break, "were your ears burning this morning?"

"No. Why?" Denise, a bit confused, asked. *Where is Natalie going with this conversation?* The look on her face revealed her thoughts.

"Your ears should have been burning," I replied. Good timing, because her current boss had just walked into the room. "Patty and I were just talking about how you are worth your weight in gold. You turned a confused and angry client into a raving fan when you got onto the phone with them at 10:30 p.m. last night. You were amazing."

Denise turned to her boss and asked, "Did you hear that?" Indeed she had.

After Denise's boss left, Denise complained, "No one tells me I'm doing a good or bad job. I don't feel appreciated."

She had really valued hearing my feedback. Denise needed to establish a vision for herself, then measure herself against the image of success. From there, capture evidence of success. But just what type of success points should Denise capture?

The challenge for most people is identifying their successes, skills, and competencies. Often these items are as elusive as the nose on your face. If you don't have a mirror, it's difficult to see your nose, yet it's right in front of you.

You can use several tools to identify your talents and skills. In particular there are tools that I've honed over the years, taking the systems my mom taught me even further. The first two serve as a foundation for discovering your talents and presenting your skills to others. These will help you confidently portray your proficiencies in a manner that resonates. Mom showed me how to build an instrument over time to showcase achievements, and that tool was called a "Brag Book."

A Brag Book is a success portfolio. This is as simple as keeping a three-ring binder or even a file folder containing compliments, past positive reviews, certificates of achievement, class completion certificates, graphs of progress, and pictures of your accomplishments. As you accumulate praises, you'll add to your portfolio over time. Lots of people also incorporate stories on LinkedIn and other platforms.

Maria, an electrical and instrumentation technician, was proud of herself and wanted to share her success with others through a post. What was impressive about the post was that she was able to summarize her project while also detailing what it took to finish it. In her post, Maria shares, "I am so proud I took on this little project and did it myself!"

Maria took before and after pictures, then described how she usually doesn't start projects like this. She had to design the electrical schematic, label wires, then make sure the new panel she put together was safe. She was proud of herself because she took the initiative to learn something new, a venture that others didn't expect her to step up to (Morena, 2022).

Creating a paragraph that mentions what steps were taken to complete the assignment, what was challenging, and why you were delighted is a great way to grow a Brag Book. You can even collect data to generate graphs of progress over time.

The Brag Book identifies the outcomes of undertakings based upon the work you've been involved with over time. In summary, these stories make up a novel that shows how you've been able to make a difference throughout your career.

Stephanie summarizes her career track by acknowledging that her vocation is far from ordinary. She was grateful for learning opportunities that had her working on multiple projects involving people from several countries. Stephanie's career path began when she accepted an engineering position, leading her to become an operations analyst. From there, she took on the role of risk management. She moved on to training, project management, and, finally, strategic accounts. From there, Stephanie became the vice president of facilities.

Stephanie shared, "After twenty-two years, I'm so excited and grateful for the opportunity to bring it all together. Next week, I'll be moving into the role of vice president of GYM (Grow Your Margins) and C-IMP (Continuous Improvement) for [my company]" (Riggs, 2022).

As a deli and grocery store owner and a nurse department leader, Mom had no problem showing her success up to that point. Still, others might have trouble deciding which experiences to include. I found the answer through a workshop put on by the Phillips ROI Institute.

The Phillips ROI Institute uses a robust system to help leaders calculate a "return on investment" for projects. You can use their approach to help determine what type of materials to save in your Brag Book.

The Phillips system identifies five different bragging rights.

**REACTIONS**

The first type of reaction we can place in the Brag Book includes emotional responses to projects or help we've provided to teams. Emotional reactions can consist of something as easy as notes of admiration you've received for the great work you've done, or survey responses executed at the end of projects. For example, we've started an Empowering Women program at my company.

We believe in the high potential of all employees, especially women. I gathered the female leaders of the organization and asked them if they would be willing to deliver talks for other women in the company. We discussed developing the program and decided on calling it Empowering Women!

We were interested in sharing the success principles that helped us grow personally and professionally through regular workshops with engaging speakers. Our mission was simple: to bring out the best leadership skills and empower the women working at our company to reach their highest potential both at work and at home.

The first workshop executed was called "The Leaders' Journey." It was well-received, according to a survey we put out. We learned that 90 percent of those who attended the program felt the workshop was beneficial. We also knew that the women who participated in the program were most pleased that having a place to voice their opinions and participate gave them a sense of value and pride in the organization. It also gave us a sense of great satisfaction for delivering value to other women.

**STATISTICS**

Another critical piece of information to add to your Brag Book is any type of improvement that resulted from your work assignments. Some statistical examples are:

- An improvement in response time when solving problems
- Reductions in turnaround time
- The number of product releases

You can then describe your part in the process of generating the improvements.

### TIMING

The speed at which a project was implemented is another story you can add to your Brag Book. For example, we learned that Sharifah needed to find a building for her organization. She had to do it in a short timeframe. Sharifah shared the timeline was aggressive, only four months, and Sharifah got it done.

### IMPACT

Another item you can add to your Brag Book is the impact a program you participated in or led had on results for the company. In 2018, the diagnostic company I was working with developed an innovative method to determine the type of antibiotic to prescribe to patients suffering from recurrent urinary tract infections (UTIs). Women suffering from recurrent UTIs have been prescribed antibiotics before test results come back. Sometimes the prescriptions either didn't work and the symptoms didn't go away, or the UTI returned within a short period of time (Spaulding, 2021).

The diagnostic testing method my company developed was shown to resolve the symptoms so that it reduced hospitalization (Daly, 2020). While we could clinically show the reduction in hospitalizations, we were unable to explain the mechanism. Based upon extensive literature searches and discussions with basic researchers worldwide, I developed a hypothesis that led to marketing pieces and a change in how we should test bacteria.

**FINANCIAL**

The last level of proof shows the cost or revenue benefit of a project. During Amanda's tenure at a university in the United States, she recalls, "I was recognized by the university's board of trustees for preparing the university's facilities and administrative rate. The university increased its financial and administrative cost rate by one point, resulting in a $4.1 million increase in federal revenue over four years."

Keeping a brag book accomplishes several important goals:

- It gives you a chance to remember all the great work you have done throughout your career. You can also use it to fill out your employee review.
- It motivates you when you are feeling down.
- It provides talking points for future interviews.

However, Mom's problem was that she didn't initiate or keep a Brag Book. Instead, she had to look back and recall stories from her past. Mom had to recreate a list of achievements from memory. She called this a "retrospective analysis." She was the first to teach me how to review historical success and move forward with future achievements.

Access bonus items such as pictures, a guided meditation, music lists, and other goodies through the QR code.

CHAPTER 7

# Analyzing Past Successes Produces Increased Confidence

*"Those who are confident believe in their capabilities, talents, and strengths."*

Mom didn't proactively build a Brag Book because she was busy running the stores, working in the emergency room, going to school, and being a mom. Like most of us women, she kept her head down and did what she needed to do to survive and work toward a dream. Building a Brag Book as she went along didn't occur to her. Mom found she had to create a book of her achievements by recalling past successes and then pulling them together into one location.

She increased her self-confidence by gathering data from her past successes via talking to others about attending medical school. Us women need to catalog our past and current accomplishments as well. Women have what it takes to succeed in leadership positions. We just need to pull our data together to prove our point to others.

Alan Benson and his colleagues analyzed data records of people working in a retail chain. They were particularly interested in learning who would be promoted and why. To understand who and why people were promoted, they analyzed yearly employee reviews and potential ratings. Overall, Benson found women were rated highly effective but were given lower potential ratings than men. The result was that women were not promoted as frequently to higher positions as men (Benson, 2021).

Benson's team found that women made up 56 percent of entry-level workers but only 14 percent of top-line district managers. Furthermore, there was no wage gap in comparing women's pay to men when working in a position at the same level. Pay gaps were generated because the women were not promoted into leadership ranks. In fact, women were 14 percent less likely to be promoted than men even though the women performed 7.3 percent better.

The retail chain promoted employees based upon their potential scores. Potential was defined as an employee's ability to contribute to the future through management or taking on greater responsibilities. The women were given potential scores 8.3 percent lower than the men.

In addition, the same women—when promoted—outperformed men at even higher levels, as evidenced by their higher performance scores during annual review periods.

After reviewing the data, Benson discovered that the men's potential scores were artificially higher than the women's because the organization feared men would leave when they were passed over for a promotion. Thus, even though the men did not perform as well as women, they were still given higher pay and more special promotions.

In interviews with women, Benson learned that they believed they shouldn't go for a promotion because they had to substantiate their abilities. But the fact is, they didn't need to confirm they were good enough: there was already evidence in their reviews that they had outperformed men. Instead, women needed the confidence to champion themselves.

As a clinical scientist, I conduct several studies, including retrospective studies. A retrospective study is one in which you gather data from the past, analyze it, and formulate a hypothesis based upon the trends you see. Google defines a hypothesis as "a supposition or proposed explanation made based upon limited evidence as a starting point for further examination." A hypothesis, in this case, refers to a belief based upon previous accomplishments that you can obtain a different or more significant position and be a success.

Studying the past and forming a hypothesis based upon evidence of past success is a powerful tool for developing an optimistic view of your future. With a Brag Book, we can confidently say, "Because I've achieved these results in that environment under those conditions, I can be the success you need under different conditions."

Ultimately, performing a retrospective study on yourself helps you gain confidence and the talking points to advocate for yourself. This self-study offers the benefits of:

- Consolidating records of success into one location.
- Measuring your accomplishments to increase your confidence in yourself.
- Using the measurements to support your positive claims about your work.
- Providing others with talking points to advocate for you when you are not in the room to speak for yourself.

Just how would you perform a retrospective analysis of your successes?

A retrospective study simply pulls together a list of projects you've completed over time. It then examines each project from five different perspectives.

First of all, it is necessary to describe the project's goals, any problems the company wanted to solve, and why the project was essential to solving those problems.

Secondly, how would the company know if they successfully achieved the objectives? This portion outlines the methods or processes you and the organization used to implement the project, collect data, and the time and cost required to execute the project.

In the next part of the report, we discuss the project's results, including how others have reacted to it and what learning has occurred within the organization.

The fourth section contains conclusions from the study and recommendations for future projects and learnings that the organization should consider moving forward.

The last section should contain tables, graphs, or testimonies.

Mom had tons to draw from to demonstrate why she would be the candidate the medical school was looking for. The school that accepted her wanted candidates who had a wide range of life experiences. The school hoped that the wide variety of backgrounds would cross-pollinate into their education and enhance their medical practice. It was evident to the school how exactly her skills matched the competencies they sought.

I used this process to transfer to a new role and get promoted all at the same time. I had attempted to shift from a medical science liaison (MSL) position to a sales director position. In the first role, I would present information and deliver talks to physicians about how molecular diagnostic tests help them diagnose their patients. I also assisted the sales team during meetings with their clients. But I wanted to move to a sales director position. As a sales director, I would lead a team in growing the business. The two were related positions but were not the same.

As an MSL, I didn't necessarily need to motivate the team to sell as I would have as a sales director. Thus, I needed to pull together a plan to show the organization and the leadership team that I could do so. I devised a promotional strategy in which the sales team would promote a talk that I would give to physicians. I then had to ensure the sales team would follow up with those physicians who attended the event and ensure the tests I promoted were ordered following the talk. Later, I tracked our success.

I captured the information outlined in the section above. Unfortunately for me, I had to gather this information after the fact. Once assembled, I created excellent charts and graphs. When the position opened up, I interviewed for a sales director position and eventually got the role. Had I not put that information together, I would not have interviewed as well.

After compiling information and reviewing your goals, your next step is to grow your confidence. Using this data is essential to increase your confidence and manage negative thoughts as you go for your dream. In chapter three, we discussed the two different parts of the brain, the positive center that assists you in dreaming and the one that helps you think critically. It's essential to manage the critical thinking portion to hold down the fear that would cause you to give up on your dream.

Mom had lots of people, especially her mother, tell her that she was making a mistake in going to medical school when she was older. However, Mom never doubted herself. I asked her about hearing grandma tell her she was getting dumber as she got older.

"Natalie, I didn't hear any of it." Mom had confidence.

You'll manage by firmly believing you have what it takes to succeed. If I have any doubts, I use those doubts to constructively prepare for success.

Carol, a managing partner for a consulting firm, shows us how to stay confident and manage fear perfectly. Carol asked her social contacts to consider that "imposter syndrome" is a good thing.

Carol shares that her past definition of imposter syndrome means to feel:

- Not confident
- Like a fraud
- No control over the situation (should something go wrong)
- Constantly doubting
- Sabotaging oneself due to limiting beliefs

Carol went on to say, "In every role I have had, despite being the best or one of the best on the sales floor, I suffered from imposter syndrome and worried that one day I would be 'found out' and my success would end. Despite that, in my career as a founder, a sales director, or a sales rep, I always stayed at the top. Not once or twice, but consecutively. Could imposter syndrome be a good thing?"

Perhaps, she was able to use her fears constructively. She used her concerns to help her become a better professional.

Carol explains, "Take an arrogant salesperson. They are good at their job, but they think they know everything. Not much new for them to learn. They tend to be a one-trick pony. If something does not go their way, they will make an excuse [and] blame the prospect."

Carol, on the other hand, discovered how to use her fear to constructively prepare for success. She shares, "I worry a lot about failure, yet I always manage to succeed. How is that possible? My worry fuels me to be great."

Carol's summary is this: "Being an 'imposter' makes you a better learner. Being confident in your abilities makes you feel good. Having both is the recipe for success" (Malakasus, 2021).

You should track your successes as a list to stay confident. Additionally, commit to taking responsibility for your thoughts. Remember that the doubts are minor blips that do not define you. Your past successes outweigh the small moments of doubt and even mistakes.

Mom analyzed her background and provided enough proof of her successes. By the time she met with the admissions board, they only had to discuss the fine points of the tasks Mom needed to complete to be admitted into the school.

Mom communicated her stories through short snippets using the STAR method, commonly found on the internet. STAR stands for situation, task, action, result. The stories you've already put together allow you to compile your accounts quickly and easily. The Brag Book will enable you to go into more depth.

By the time you've pulled this information together, you'll not fall into the same trap of feeling you are not ready for your next step.

Even if you feel you are not ready for a promotion or the transfer, Mom advises you to try to apply for the position anyway.

Chances are that by applying for the transition or promotion, you may get to the next level earlier than you expect. You will discover that you were indeed ready.

Mom applied to thirteen medical schools and interviewed with two of them. She was accepted into one. Mom could have let the fact that she didn't hear back or was rejected from eleven of the thirteen schools get her down. Her ongoing faith in her ability to get into a medical school taught me how to stay resilient when setbacks happen.

Access bonus items such as pictures, a guided meditation, music lists, and other goodies through the QR code.

CHAPTER 8

# Networking-Connecting Visions

---

"There is one big 'why' that drives each worthwhile goal."

Beverly let those she worked and went to school with know she was interested in applying to medical school. One professor, Sister Amelia, encouraged her. Sister Amelia let Bevie know that she saw talent in her, telling her, "Bevie, you are an excellent problem solver. You have it in you to go all the way." Mom asked Sister Amelia to write a recommendation letter on her behalf, and Sister Amelia was more than willing. Beverly also spoke with new residents about their process of getting into and going through medical school. With each conversation, Mom learned more.

I had to take Mom's example and build upon it in my career, knowing that men get ahead by employing the motto, "Who you know is more important than what you know." Our motto should be, "Who you know is important, and they should know your talent and be willing to tell others about it." Your potential is directly tied to what you've done, how you think, your work ethic, and your ability to collect and motivate a team. They should recognize what you can do for a company or group of investors in the future with all that power.

In the end, our job is to deliver results that make a difference. The bottom line is that we need to think about how we are moving "the needle forward."

What does moving the needle forward mean? It's a phrase we often hear in business.

Picture the speed gauges in your car that indicate you're accelerating, staying at the same speed, or slowing. The little tick marks and the arrow help you know where you are relative to a goal, whether in range, below, or above. In our business case, the zero mark is the start of the project or program, and the maximum speed is the end. When we think about a project or a business goal, we typically begin at zero with a complete plan to the right at maximum. We have a specific time to start from zero and hit the maximum.

Our responsibility is to push the pointer forward tick by tick, project by project, within a specific time frame until we reach the "maximum" and complete the assignment. However, as all great stories show, conflict abounds, and it's normal to encounter problems. One tick may introduce more complications than another when "moving the needle"—pay attention to those moments. How you help move the needle when it gets stuck are opportunities for you to shine. Your story comes about from your ability to solve problems when they arise and hitting the goal on time as a result.

It's imperative to learn how to comfortably share your story—it's a part of networking. People love to hear good news, and you have great information to share.

Josie was a high-powered advertising executive leading a technical marketing team at a sizable diagnostic company. Viewing her as a respected leader, the organization asked Josie to mentor young women in the corporation so that the organization could gain more talent over time. Josie encouraged her mentees that higher leadership levels are available for them.

She would also tell them, "Share what you're doing with people in a palatable way." Josie would then lay out how to do so. "You need to remind your boss of the good things you've done and be results-oriented, not action-oriented."

We leaders understand that many people are fearful of being result-oriented and are instead action-oriented. To produce results, you must think about what you are doing, why you are taking action, and adjust as you accumulate new data. In other words, Josie continues, "Get shit done, #GSD, that pushes the needle forward. It's not easy."

Her point is significant.

Josie expands, "People will tell the boss, for example, 'I've conducted twenty-five phone calls today,' and they want a pat on the back. But what the boss needs to know is, 'What did you do that moved the needle forward?' Tell the boss about the results of the twenty-five telephone calls. Your boss should know where the organization was before and where it is now after the action."

I agree with Josie about confirming you understand the purpose of your work and knowing how your actions are driving positive consequences for the company. Additionally, it's essential to stay balanced.

Early in my career, I was a little over-the-top in trying to produce positive outcomes. My health suffered because of my high-level drive and so did the emotional health of my family.

I have observed other high-level women and men sometimes falling into the trap of driving for results by disrespectfully conveying their directives, all for pushing others to get things done.

Running over others is not what Josie means about driving for results and moving the needle forward.

Overusing the strength of "driving for results" can cause you to be described as a "bull in a china shop." This type of person shows no regard for processes, constantly creating shortcuts and triggering problems for bosses to clean up.

I've managed these types of sales representatives.

At first, I was happy we were producing sales and growing the business. The results were great; however, the dead bodies piled up to the point where I couldn't ignore that we had an issue. (I use "dead bodies" to refer to the operational folks who burned out trying to please the few salespeople with several unusual requests.)

I also discovered there were tons of broken promises made to customers. The salespeople who overused the "drive for results" had promised services we could not deliver; customers were unhappy and disenchanted with our company. Not good.

How does an appropriate and balanced "drive for results" and "moving the needle forward" relate to networking?

Networking is about connecting: that is, connecting with others and their goals. In other words, networking is about boldly dreaming, sharing your dream, and explaining how you are going about achieving it…while also learning about other people's dreams. Once the two parties know each other's goals and objectives, it's about creating connections between the visions and exploring how to achieve them together. Thus, when you network, you connect your drive and other people's drive for balanced results.

When talking about your goals while networking, you should tell people what type of results you intend to achieve and how your actions will benefit them. Explain the change you want to complete in the future.

I took Mom's experiences to heart because she spoke with others about her dream. Because of her, I've been open with my own dreams.

Dream. Know your intentions, meaning, and what type of difference you want to make in the world.

When I was interested in transferring and receiving a promotion from an individual producer as a medical science liaison to a sales director, I seized opportunities to speak with others about my goal. I conversed with sales representatives, asking them to provide stories of sales directors that helped them achieve their greatest successes. I was curious about what they needed from a leader to help them succeed.

I set up lunches with current professionals in the role to discover the types of challenges they encountered and how they worked to achieve the best results despite problems. I was curious: What would I face in that role? What were the best ways to manage its challenges?

I chatted with my boss about my hope of being a sales director one day. I did so while also staying diligent in my current role. My attentiveness to my work while also having transparent conversations, in the end, paid off.

When beginning the networking process to achieve your career goals, there are several reasons to start with your boss. She can assign you projects that help you develop your skills. These projects may also cause you to gain access to the people you need to network with. Additionally, she may be aware of positions opening in the organization before they are announced. In those cases, she can sponsor you for informal interviews before the jobs are advertised.

The organization will be willing to assist you because your promotion increases employee engagement, making your boss look good. When employee engagement increases, your boss's scorecard points increase too.

The question is: How do you network with your boss and gain her commitment to helping you achieve your goals in a way that also projects loyalty?

You can introduce the topic during a regular meeting or as part of an employee review. This is your chance to let your boss know what you enjoy most about your work. Having said that, you can let her know you would like to be more involved in the organization by utilizing these skills in a deeper or more meaningful way in the future. Explain to your boss the direction in which you intend to take your career.

Ask your boss if she would consider:

- Helping you both to cocreate a developmental plan to improve critical competencies that are important in your current and future roles. Know you must take the initiative.
- Creating a network plan to help you get in front of key people.
- Offering projects that you could lead that would assist the boss in her role while also preparing you for the next level.

While you should reassure the manager that your goal is to ensure her success, you should also outline the steps you will take to stay focused on your current job.

I've only had one boss not willing to partner with me. He was unusual. All my other bosses were ready to help me at this stage of the game.

The next collaboration meeting you will need to conduct is with potential hiring managers. You do not have to wait for an opening; instead, the hiring managers need to know you are interested in any soon-to-be open positions. Ask for a networking meeting by letting the manager know you would like to conduct an informational meeting with them because you would like to learn more about various departments.

Give folks a clear sense of what you want to accomplish now and in the future by presenting a crisp opening. Gain permission to ask questions. Ensure you stay on track during these informal networking sessions, and don't run over the allotted time.

Practice an elevator speech which states what you're doing now, what you would like to do in the future, and the type of contribution you want to make to the organization. The three sentences must be very concise.

One of the companies I worked in sent a group of us to a year-long women's development program. There, we were taught to ask leading questions centered around the company's goals and the most prominent challenges it would face in the immediate future.

Related questions you can ask leaders during the meetings include:

- How does the department affect the company?
- What is the vision or goal of the department? What are the results the company is interested in achieving?
- What are the biggest challenges the department and the organization face now?
- What do you expect the biggest challenges the organization will face in the future to be?
- What skill sets will the staff need to meet the challenges?

After answering these questions, again, let the individual know you are scheduling these types of informational interviews with many people throughout the organization. Let them know about your interest in moving forward in the company and ask if it is okay to keep in contact.

Those who network well would encourage you to give a few ideas during these discussions. For example, suppose you were in the medical industry and in the middle of a pandemic like COVID-19. In that case, you could come to the meeting with thoughts on how you can support the company by resolving employee burnout. Offer ideas so that these leaders learn more about how you think.

Our development program also instructed us to follow the discussion up by writing a thank you note. You would be amazed how many people don't write thank you letters.

Interestingly, when we met with various leaders, we heard a lot of information about the big picture as we moved up to meet the CEO and senior vice presidents. We also learned about large-scale changes that the organization would most likely face in the future due to the shifting market.

One strategy for streamlining the meeting is to join forces with other like-minded individuals in the organization. Plan the discussion together. I encourage you to ensure you set up the appointments although it seems daunting. Suppose the hiring manager knows you are meeting with these other people. In that case, they will more than likely remember you when it comes time to interview.

The tactics described so far in the book discuss the interviews you should conduct in your own organization. The same questions can be asked in interviews conducted outside your current corporation.

Mom met with several high-profile people within the university she was attending. The people she met referred her to other people, which led to her receiving a high-level recommendation letter to medical school. Networking helped Mom increase her confidence and chances for acceptance and success.

Access bonus items such as pictures, a guided meditation, music lists, and other goodies through the QR code.

## CHAPTER 9

# Dealing with Setbacks

---

*"The trick to becoming more confident is to set a goal, break it down, stay accountable, work on your fears, prepare for failure, and don't quit."*

Mom applied to several different medical schools; however, every one of the local schools sent her a rejection letter. Mom contacted the schools that had denied her application to learn why they would not admit her. Unfortunately, the local schools did not return her calls.

Mom could have responded by giving up after the schools' rejections; for example, she could have taken the refusals personally, feeling bad about herself. She could have believed that the snub was her fault and that she wasn't meant to have such a big dream. I would have heard her say, "It was stupid for me to apply; what was I thinking?"

It's such an important point to not criticize yourself or give up when you are rejected. It's also important not to believe "I can't."

As an adult, I compete on several tennis teams. To ensure I'm at my best, I take lessons from one of the top tennis coaches in the area. Lucky for me, the best female teenage tennis players also take lessons right next to my practice court. From time to time, I get to watch them between points or as I'm picking up tennis balls between training drills. These teenagers are outstanding players. It's inspiring to watch how hard and accurately they hit the ball.

One day, they played an intense tennis match against one another. Lots of grunting, running, and harder hitting than usual. The points seemed to last forever.

Then, one of the girls said something under her breath. The coach didn't like what he heard, stopped the match, and yelled, "What did you say?"

Red-faced and ashamed, the girl responded, "Nothing."

The coach wouldn't let it go. "No, I heard you. What did you say?" I thought maybe she'd said a naughty swear word. Sheepishly the girl said, "I didn't say anything." Again, the coach wouldn't let it go.

My coach and I were bystanders. Amazed and wide-eyed, I asked my coach, "Geeze, what did she say? It must be awful?" It was then what she said came out.

She had said, "I can't." And it was indeed a terrible thing to say.

With that, the coach and the teen's father pulled her aside and had an intense discussion together. They wouldn't tolerate the thought of "I can't."

I never heard my mother criticize herself, her intellect, or her self-belief. I never overheard her say, "I can't."

I couldn't imagine such a statement ever coming from her. She'd heard it from me when I felt rejected. Mom's response was always, "Natalie, that's stinking thinking. Stop it right now."

Mom also could have felt flawed, thinking that no other medical school would accept her even outside of the local area. The key was for her to stay calm and know she was going through a learning process.

What kept Mom motivated to continue applying even after she received rejection letters, and most schools didn't want to discuss her candidacy with her?

Mom intuitively knew that she would eventually be accepted into a program. Mom understood, with enough feedback, that she could adjust her application to make it more robust in the future.

Having faith paid off. She kept applying to medical schools and contacting any school that rejected her. One of the schools that said no to her candidacy called her back to provide feedback. It turned out that her transcript was missing one of the required prerequisite classes.

Mom asked their administration, "If I take the class in the summer, would you accept me for medical school?" Their answer was an affirmative, "Yes!"

It's a good thing my mom had a positive mindset, knowing that she would attend medical school at some point. She viewed every rejection as an opportunity to learn. Had Mom taken rejection personally, she would not have called that school to ask what was needed. She wouldn't have known that it was just a matter of taking one more class.

It turns out that the medical school Mom was accepted into was a perfect institution for her. As you know, the school had decided that they were interested in training a different type of physician. They wanted to attract older students with diverse backgrounds. For example, they accepted pharmacists, nurses like my mom, and other students with work experience in the medical field. If Mom hadn't worked through the setbacks, she would not have continued to apply, call the administrative boards, and push through the obstacles to achieve success.

Mom retaining faith in herself instead of reacting to negative messages caused her to exercise emotional resilience. Instead of becoming depressed and internalizing discouraging messages, she became curious. That curiosity made the difference and gave her a choice to keep going.

As with anything new, things go wrong; you can always count on failing. Many things can go awry within a career, including not getting a job, being eliminated from a company, missing deadlines, giving a poor presentation, losing a big customer, getting a bad review, or even being fired.

When things go wrong, there are many ways to deal with the fallout. You could let the perceived failure define you, believing that you "can't" have success. You could blame others and have a resentful attitude. You could also have faith in yourself and constructively learn from the rejection.

What helps anyone to get back up and try again? It's important to know that the failures don't define you unless you let them.

Take Mom's advice. Choose to have faith in yourself, have optimism for the future, and become curious when things don't work out.

Having faith in yourself is as simple as revisiting your vision. You've imagined the best future you would like to put into place, and that vision excites you. Reviewing that future is the key to overcoming failure.

Your highest self believes in your ability to succeed and embodies hope with a positive outlook.

Women striving to become their highest self are engaged, and that engagement brings about work success. Just as Mom had an inner knowing that she would successfully enter medical school, so she became deeply involved in applying. She sought to learn every step of the way, even when rejected.

Kathleen Buse and Diana Bilimoria conducted a study to understand how and when women persist in STEM careers. They interviewed both engineering women who left the profession and those who had longevity. Women leave the engineering profession at a higher rate than any other occupation.

The main reason women leave their careers is that the work environment is filled with barriers and discrimination. Yet, despite the difficulties, some women don't quit and actually thrive. Buse and Bilimoria wanted to understand the power of vision in helping women stay in the field. They wanted to know about each woman's ideal self during the interviews, asking, "What would they wish to occur in their career?"

They found that the women that stayed in engineering had a vision of what they wanted to do or be in the future. The women had their ideal selves in mind. Those that left the profession tended to move in a direction that fit their perfect self. These women intentionally changed toward a different life by developing their needed skills to create and sustain that change. Those who stayed in the harsh environment, too, had a vision. Their vision was to survive and thrive in the engineering environment. They developed the skills to sustain an engineering career (Buse, 2014).

Like the engineering women, reviewing your vision is very important and is the secret to staying resilient during obstacles. It is easier to recover when faced with difficulties if you remember the victory you plan to experience when you achieve the goal.

Visualizing is very simple and can be done anywhere and anytime. It's as simple as picturing yourself in the future, being your best self.

While you've established your vision, revisiting it is essential. The brain is naturally driven to keep you safe. All the hopeful, warm, fuzzy feelings you experienced when you initially created your dream will dissipate over time. Rejection ignites the fear centers of your psyche, causing your imagination to drift even further from your goal.

The antidote is to consistently meditate and revisit your aspirations. From time to time, Vishen Lakhiani, founder of Mindvalley, offers free vision courses which provide a framework for daily active meditation. According to Vishien, you must visualize the future you want three years from now, then picture how you will achieve the vision each day (Lakhiani, 2020).

Midway through my career, I wanted to become a sales director. At that point, I was employed by a large company. I was very keen about moving from my current sales specialist to a sales director position. This step was an upward move through the organization. As I have explained, I had been exercising indirect leadership skills by helping sales generalists promote a line of technically challenging diagnostic tests. My role was to assist in the sales process, educate the generalists, and motivate them to help promote the diagnostic assays I presented to clients. I loved the leadership and influence aspects of my job. I desired to have an opportunity to employ more of those types of skills.

I knew that if I moved into the director role, I would get to execute my leadership skills. I imagined myself in a more prominent leadership role. I knew that I could do good for the company, employees, and corporation in the sales director's position.

I developed and executed a plan to move beyond the role of my current sales specialist position.

I interviewed current directors to learn more about what was required to succeed in the director role. I met informally with leaders to let them know I was interested. I demonstrated my ability to complete the job during interviews. I expressed my passion for the position and hopes of entering it one day.

Furthermore, I asked for the leaders' commitment to remembering that I wanted to pursue the role. I found a mentor who happened to be my boss's boss to help me during the interview process. I executed this plan with the blessing of my immediate supervisor.

The day finally arrived, and I interviewed for a director position. While I made it to the final round of interviews, I did not get the job.

Shortly after that, a second director position opened, and again, while I was prepared, I did not get that position either.

In the alternate case, a person with more experience than me triumphed and got the job.

I was sad about not receiving the job twice and was quite depressed. Unlike my mom, I felt terrible. I felt dismissed for corporate political reasons beyond my control. I also worried that my advanced degree, in this case, hurt my chances of success.

I almost gave up. I didn't want to return to work. I didn't know what to say to my co-worker friends when they asked what happened.

However, there was a tiny spark of hope in me. Due to my visioning work, I knew that it was part of my purpose in life to one-day move to that role. I held that kernel of hope and belief as a mustard seed. Intuitively, I had an inner feeling that I would get the job. I knew the tiny mustard seed would turn into a tree.

After the second rejection, I called my mentor to discuss the situation so that I could turn the corner and learn constructively from the case.

Unfortunately, I knew it was about to get ugly because of how he answered the phone.

"Ya," he said gruffly.

"I guess you already heard?" Up to that point, I had only felt support from those around me, including my mentor.

"Natalie, I told you not to go for the position. You've been rejected now twice. You know what people are saying about you now, right?"

"No, what do you mean?"

"You're making a fool of yourself. If you're not going to listen to me, I'm not going to mentor you anymore." He abruptly hung up the phone.

Dumbfounded, I thought, *Wow! That was not the conversation I expected.*

At the time of the telephone call, I was sitting in an airport Chili's restaurant on the way home from a business trip.

Chips, salsa, and Diet Coke sat in front of me. My next thought was, *I need something stronger.*

I called the waitress over. "I'll have a beer, please!"

I reflected on that confusing reaction. *I wonder what's up with him?*

Deep breath. I had to revisit my vision. *If not this path, then what else is there?*

Suddenly, my faith grew. I knew this would be the path I would take at some point. I needed to learn from Mom. I needed to handle the rejection by staying in faith and not taking anything personally.

The fact that Mom was rejected so many times when applying to medical school inspired me. With each rejection, she learned something and followed up by either fine tuning the search or taking more classes. As she discovered new things and did more, she eventually succeeded in getting into medical school. Likewise, I felt that I, too, was learning.

Despite my mentor's warning, I felt guided to continue trying for a similar role. I persisted because I had done my homework and decided I must follow my passion.

I knew I was pursuing the right dream in my heart, and I couldn't immediately drop it. I was confident that something would get ironed out in my favor over time. I wouldn't let the dream die as my mentor had just advised. I had a fire in my heart that would not be snuffed out.

And then, the faith in myself in making my aspirations a reality finally paid off!

Within six weeks, I received phone calls from two different leaders within the organization asking if I was interested in interviewing for two distinct sales leadership positions. It was as if the universe was giving my negative mentor the middle finger for discouraging me! Ha!

It turned out that the person initially hired over me for one of the positions had quit within two weeks. Additionally, a different position also opened. I was now offered a choice to move into one of two different roles, one which required moving and the other that did not.

I chose the path that required moving higher up in the company because it offered stocks and was more challenging.

Staying true to my vision paid off. The idea wasn't alive just in my head; it was also in my heart. The power of persistence, knowing the importance of aligning your thoughts with your gut and staying true to your higher self, leads to sticking with it and attaining success.

A little over a decade later, the mentor who dumped me and told me I was making a fool of myself contacted me about another position he had open at the time. He had moved to a different company and had an opening that he thought would be a good fit for me. He said, "Natalie, I've watched your career with great interest. I've learned from your successes that I needed to stay out of your way." That was a remarkable statement.

After the call, I realized that I've learned how to walk through glass walls like Mom.

Access bonus items such as pictures, a guided meditation, music lists, and other goodies through the QR code located below.

**CHAPTER 10**

# Pulling It All Together

---

*"The mind is everything. What you think, you become."*

THE BUDDHA

Mom's steps for walking through glass walls started with her belief in herself and her positive vision for the future. When faced with criticism, she held two opposing ideas in her head: knowing she would succeed and compassion for the naysayers.

She didn't let our patriarchal society determine her role in the world; instead, she paid attention to the spark of inspiration that first lit itself in her heart. Mom let the spark grow to a full-on vision that fueled her passion for delivering positive results for her patients and society.

Mom realized there would never be a perfect time or perfect conditions in which she should pursue her vision. Yet, she also realized nothing was stopping her. She created a plan to reach her goals, beginning with reviewing her competencies and learning how to tell her success story. From there, she networked with others to understand the challenges she would face and learn from their experiences on how to overcome the difficulties.

She also developed a team of leaders who would speak positively about her.

When it seemed her dreams were fading, as schools were rejecting her and not returning her calls, Mom held firm to her belief that she would get into medical school. Mom did not give up. She revisited her vision and stuck with the plan.

Mom's blueprint for success worked, and those who were initially unhappy with the announcement that we had to relocate to another state were proud of her. Everyone was excited to attend her graduation ceremony.

My brother, sister, and I all attended college. Beyond that, all three of us succeeded in post-graduate work as well: me with a PhD, my brother with two master's degrees, and my sister with a master's degree and aspirations to earn a PhD too!

Additionally, all three of us have moved up the career ladder in the companies for which we were employed. Mom's formula helped all three of us succeed.

The question is: Will Mom's formula also make a difference for you?

In the right environment, yes.

In the wrong environment, possibly not.

My husband and I had dinner at our favorite Chinese restaurant down the street from our house a few years ago. We were weekly regulars and were escorted to our informally assigned booth. Rather than sitting across from one another, we enjoyed sitting next to each other. Since we were frequent visitors, we generally had the same waiter, Chin-Hae. Even though the restaurant served Chinese food, Chin-Hae was born and raised in Korea and had recently moved to the United States.

We enjoyed learning about South Korean culture from Chin-Hae, especially since my husband was born in Korea and adopted by United States parents as a toddler. We found learning about a new culture fascinating. While we were both very fond of Chin-Hae, I'm not sure he cared for me so much because, as a woman, I didn't obey the Korean societal rules. During one of our evenings, my husband cracked what I thought was a funny joke, and I put a hand on my husband's shoulder and laughed along with him.

Chin-Hae's face turned red as he angrily informed me, "You can't touch your husband's shoulder like that."

Confused, I asked, "Why not?"

"Because," said Chin-Hae, shocked I didn't understand, "it's a sign of equality. Women are not equal to men." He then said, "If your husband was truly Korean, he would never have married you."

My answer was: "That's fine because if he was to ask me to obey the rules you've outlined, I wouldn't have married him either."

Later, as mentioned earlier in this book, I learned that the pay gap between women and men in Korea is the highest in the world, 31.8 percent.

Only 1.8 percent of Korean-owned companies have a woman sitting in the CEO seat. In most cases, she's there only because the company is family owned and the family doesn't have a son. Only 2.7 percent of women are found on the next rung of leaders and hold a vice president's role (Cho, 2018).

Research shows that two cultural factors fence women in their careers, including the notion that the women's domain is the home. According to Confucianism, women were to take roles and positions below the men.

It was a beautiful summer day when my family and I decided to kayak on the river. Except I needed to take the canoe instead of a kayak like everyone else. The kayaks moved quickly on the river, cutting through it nicely; I had to paddle in the canoe much faster to keep up.

Matters worsened when I ran into a patch of river grass. River grass floats on the top of the river, and the patch I ran into was very thick. I had to work hard to power beyond. While paddling as hard and fast as possible, I only moved forward inches. By the time I made it through the grass, the rest of the family had traveled far up the river and were headed home. They'd had no troubles, while I toiled in the muck!

Working in an organization blind to its internal biases against women is like rowing through a patch of river grass. As hard as you work, it seems like you are not moving forward.

Nola was a nurse employed in the emergency room of a suburban hospital in a large metropolitan area in the United States. Nola spent years preparing herself for a leadership position in the hospital by obtaining a master's degree and earning several certifications. It wasn't easy: Nola juggled school, work, and being a mom to two beautiful girls.

After toiling in the department for over fifteen years, an opportunity finally arrived. The department opened a position for the leadership role she dreamed of and had worked years to prepare for. Ultimately, however, Nola wasn't chosen. A young man with only a bachelor's degree, two years of experience, and no certificates got the promotion instead of her.

Nola asked the leadership team to explain why they chose the young man over her. Their reason was, "They had a feeling about him." Nola immediately left the department, transferring to a different part of the organization.

When females operate in male-dominated careers, they run into a "glass ceiling" that stops their career progress into higher managerial roles. Nevertheless, when a male performs a typical female-dominated duty such as teaching, nursing, or social work, they are quickly escorted to higher levels of management. Men are escorted up the "glass elevator" primarily because management views the men as more competent leaders or fear losing the men if a woman is promoted above them. After all, management deems the masculine as more proficient (Williams, 2013).

More recent research reveals that the "glass elevator" applies more to straight, white men and less to those of a minority race or in the LGBTQ+ community. Moreover, the glass elevator and glass ceiling apply most directly to corporations that operate with a much more traditional hierarchy (Connell, 2012).

Kristen Schilt examined the career trajectory of white trans men in the work environment. The people that Schilt spoke with had lived and functioned as females before transitioning to living as men. These individuals had at first believed they would be either terminated or mocked after their transition.

Instead, Schilt discovered that most of the trans men, in fact, profited from the change. Rather than being mocked or fired, they were viewed as more proficient, given more authority, and rewarded financially in contrast with their previous life as women (Schilt, 2011).

Nola's department suffered as a result of hiring the young man over her. He only lasted two years in the advanced role before leaving the organization. On the other hand, Nola was promoted in her new department and was able to negotiate boundaries as to the hours she would be expected to work to better balance her home life.

As for Korea, while many Korean-owned companies have held women back, there are multinational companies in which Korean women excel. Multinational companies have satellite businesses located around the world. In multinational companies, 60 percent of executive positions are held by women even though they are located in Korea (Cho, 2018).

What explains the difference between the percentage of women at the top of locally owned, non-multinational Korean companies and those that are multinational?

One crucial difference is that the organization's structure and values positively impact women's ability to reach upper leadership roles. The women in the Korean multinational companies belonged to organizations that provided a system for advancement. In contrast, the locally owned companies didn't value women. Therefore, they ignored their talent, considering the women and their abilities worthless. No matter how hard they worked in the local organization, the women could rarely get ahead. In the multi-nationally run companies, women were valued, and a structure was put in place to help them get promoted.

In addition to the multinational companies being open to women in leadership roles and offering structured development programs, the women in these Korean multinational companies had several characteristics in common. This is key! Consistent with O'Neil and associates (2015), those who transformed their careers were self-confident, could take the initiative and complete projects, influence others, and were authentic. In interviews, they described their leadership styles as engaging, interactive, caring, and empowering of others.

Additionally, the women who moved up the corporate ladder held various positions within the company before becoming CEO. Their jobs ranged from sales and marketing to customer service, operations, and human resources before becoming CEO. Based on their successful career paths, we can expect to engage in the process my mom taught us several times in our careers. Likely, though, as we employ her procedure, each round will become more accessible and manageable.

Before joining an organization, it's essential to ask questions that will reveal any blind bias toward women. You can ask for examples of times when the hiring manager provided employees with growth opportunities. You can ask about formal programs available for leadership growth. You may also ask about times when projects failed. How did the organization respond to mistakes? Ask for examples of how they have recognized and rewarded employees and opened career doors for them. The answers to these questions will reveal much about their workplace environment.

Companies benefit in several ways when women are in top management positions and are on the board of directors. Studies have found a positive correlation between improved profits and stockholder value with increased women in top management positions. Additionally, companies that included women on the board of directors also had increased returns on assets and investments compared to those with only men (de Luis-Carnicer, 2008). As well as increasing profits, the inclusion of women also reduces companies' legal and operational risks due to their attention to detail and ability to ask questions from a different perspective (Adhikari, 2019).

As a result of reading this book, you have the tools to overcome the obstacles, be they internal or external, that hold women back from shattering barriers. First, you understand the basics of the patriarchal rules that cause people to become biased against women. Knowing the rules and those biases allow you to recognize and move beyond them.

Your visioning work enables you to aim higher than you otherwise would have if you had not taken the time to understand your goals. Once you've pinpointed your career objectives, you've then identified transferable skills that will help hiring managers see you as a good fit for the role. This gives you confidence as you let people inform others how you would like to grow yourself. You will develop a network plan and find a mentor two levels ahead of you to help you get to the next level.

Once you reach your new position, it's vital to succeed, bringing results to the organization. You'll need to continue adding to your Brag Book, showing success and achievements. The achievements can take many forms: monetary, cultural, and transformative.

As you succeed, and over time, your interest may change as regularly as your desires for career growth. I often view a career path as traveling on the road. Circumstantial changes are like hitting a fork in the road. Revising your vision to contemplate a new future while considering your current situation and varying interests is essential. In reviewing the new future, you can use your Brag Book as a method by which you can show transitional skills to move your career in a new direction. Using this definition leads us to view job security as not working in the same position at the same company year after year. Job security in this context is the ability to always find a job as a result of your past achievements and the vision you bring to the table.

My mom will tell you she didn't do anything special; she was just following the path that made the most sense to her. Yet, she taught me so much by following her dream.

I hope you, too, dare to dream and then pursue your ambitions. Grow, so you can inspire others with the power of your imagination and do good for the world. My prayer is that you make a maximum positive difference in helping others. Aspire to reach your highest self and do so by achieving greatness one step at a time! You will be an inspiration to your children like my mother was to me.

Access bonus items such as pictures, a guided meditation, music lists, and other goodies through the QR code located below.

# Acknowledgments

So many people helped transform this book from a thought to a physical thing! In addition to my mom, Dr. Beverly Heinking, I'd like to acknowledge my husband who spent hours listening to me as I hit obstacles in my career, challenged me when I was satisfied with the status quo, and helped me form a vision of a future that was so far above what I could imagine. Beyond that, I'd like to thank my super supporter, Shuguang Huang. Thank you, Shuguang, you are a supporter of several very intelligent and wise women. Thanks to Salina Rivera for starting me on the project. There were several people who made sure this book was an awesome product, including Mary Ceccanese, Jacquie Vealey, Abha Gulati, Joanne Gaines, and Professor Eric Koester. Thank you to my family, including Amanda Jobes, Bonnie Heinking, Julie Heinking, and Emily Heinking. Thank you to my tennis friends and sisters, including Robyn Parrott, Nancy Lamers, Joanne Gaines, Sheryl Eckert, and Jean Julian. Thank you to those for whom I've worked with, including Shawna Ramey, Cory Dunn, Deepika Bhagwat, Martin Weitzman, Carrie McGehee, Craig Simms, Kathleen Adams, Pamela Delbridge, Robert Embree, Jim Canfield, Tiina Sepp, Stephanie Ducker,

Patrick Turner, and Jennifer Mathis. Last, I'd like to thank Carolyn Marengere, Matt Alfaro, and Lauren Yodzio Gil for your support in this project.

# Appendix

---

**INTRODUCTION**

Bleidorn, Wiebke, Ruben C. Arslan, Jaap JA Denissen, Peter J. Rentfrow, Jochen E. Gebauer, Jeff Potter, and Samuel D. Gosling. "Age and gender differences in self-esteem—A cross-cultural window." *Journal of personality and social psychology* 111, no. 3 (2016): 396.

Guzman, Jorge, and Aleksandra Olenka Kacperczyk. "Gender gap in entrepreneurship." *Research Policy* 48, no. 7 (2019): 1666–1680.

Itty, Sarin Sajan, Jose Rafael Garcia, Calvin Futterman, Sofia Garcia Austt, and B. G. Mujtaba. "Breaking the glass ceiling philosophy and reality: A study of gender Progress and career development in the corporate world." Business Ethics and Leadership, Volume 3, Issue 3, (2019).

## CHAPTER 1

Dorrance Hall, Elizabeth, and Patricia E. Gettings. "'Who is this little girl they hired to work here?': Women's experiences of marginalizing communication in male-dominated workplaces." *Communication Monographs* 87, no. 4 (2020): 484–505.

Ganiyu, R. A., Oluwafemi, A., Ademola, A. A. and Olatunji, O. I., "The Glass Ceiling Conundrum: Illusory Belief or Barriers That Impede Women's Career Advancement in the Workplace." *Journal of Evolutionary Studies in Business*, vol. 3, no. 1, pp. 137–66, 2016.

"Goober's Replacement." *The Andy Griffith Show*, season 6, episode 28, CBS, March 28, 1966. IMDb. https://www.imdb.com/title/tt0053479/.

Hankyoreh. 2014. "Since 2000, S. Korea number one in OECD for gender pay inequality" https://www.hani.co.kr/arti/english_edition/e_international/649886.html.

Kim, Hunmin, *Culture and Gender in Leadership, Perspectives from the Middle East and Asia*, pp. 253–74, 2013.

Patterson, Jamal. "Equality for South Korean Women in 2020." https://www.borgenmagazine.com/equality-for-south-korean-women-in-2020/.

Ryan, Michelle K., S. Alexander Haslam, Thekla Morgenroth, Floor Rink, Janka Stoker, and Kim Peters. "Getting on top of the glass cliff: Reviewing a decade of evidence, explanations, and impact." *The Leadership Quarterly* 27, no. 3 (2016): 446–455.

"U.S. Medical School Applicants and Students 1982–1983 to 2011–2012." *aamc.org* (Report). AAMC. Archived from the original on 26 June 2014. Retrieved 9 October 2021. https://www.exercise-science-guide.com/wp-content/uploads/U.S.-Medical-School-Applicants-and-Students-1982-83-to-2011-2012.pdf

Williams, Christine L. "The glass escalator: Hidden advantages for men in the 'female' professions." *Social problems* 39, no. 3 (1992): 253–267.

Yu, JungJa Joy, and Rosemary Radford Ruether. *Breaking the Glass Box: a Korean Woman's Experiences of Conscientization and Spiritual Formation*. Wipf & Stock, 2013.

## CHAPTER 2

AAMC. "Medical Students, Selected Years." 2016. https://www.aamc.org/system/files/reports/1/2015table1.pdf.

Cole, Stephen. "Sex discrimination and admission to medical school, 1929-1984." *American Journal of Sociology* 92, no. 3 (1986): 549–567.

Downing, Capris. "Obtaining my PMP in April after months of studying, with a." LinkedIn. October 2021. https://www.linkedin.com/posts/caprisdowning_motherhood-workingmom-projectmanagement-activity-6846847643105157120-cf4E/?utm_source=linkedin_share&utm_medium=member_desktop_web.

Meyburg, Angella. "A Common Struggle for Women in the Workplace—Setting Boundaries." LinkedIn, April 1, 2021. https://

www.linkedin.com/pulse/common-struggle-women-workplace-setting-boundaries-angela-meyburg/.

Pianta, Rebecca. "Female superintendents' self-sabotaging behaviors and their journey to reclaiming their power." PhD diss., Brandman University, 2020.

Shi, Shyvee. "How did I transition from TPM to Senior Product Manager as a mid-career professional?" LinkedIn. October 2021. https://www.linkedin.com/posts/shyveeshi_productmanagement-midcareertransition-activity-6851534754878234625-auxi?utm_source=linkedin_share&utm_medium=member_desktop_web.

## CHAPTER 3

Amuah, Hazel Berrard. "The Essence of Values, Vision and Mission to the Personal Career Planning and the Essence for the Working Professional." SSRN Electronic Journal, 2012.

Boyatzis, Richard E., Kylie Rochford, and Scott N. Taylor. "The role of the positive emotional attractor in vision and shared vision: Toward effective leadership, relationships, and engagement." *Frontiers in Psychology* (2015): 670.

Forbes. "50 Over 50." 2021. https://www.forbes.com/500ver50/?profile=kim-ng.

Heaphy, Emily D., and Jane E. Dutton. "Positive social interactions and the human body at work: Linking organizations and physiology." *Academy of management review* 33, no. 1 (2008): 137–162.

Ross, Marie-Claire. "5 Reasons Why Mission-Driven Leaders are the Most Successful." https://www.linkedin.com/pulse/5-reasons-why-mission-driven-leaders-most-successful-ross-gaicd/.

## CHAPTER 4

Ajumobi, Tomi. "I quit my job in July 2020. At the time, I had been stressed." LinkedIn, July 2021. https://www.linkedin.com/feed/update/urn:li:activity:6852231790816440320/.

Bernstein, Gabby. "Gabby." 2018. https://gabbybernstein.com/feeling-good-every-day/.

## CHAPTER 5

Higgins, Alexander G. "U.N.: 100,000 Refugees Flee Iraq Monthly." News. 2006. https://web.archive.org/web/20070904002020/http:/www.boston.com/news/world/middleeast/articles/2006/11/03/un_nearly_100000_flee_iraq_monthly/.

Indeed Editorial Team. "Indeed." 2021. https://www.indeed.com/career-advice/resumes-cover-letters/transferable-skills.

World Education Services. "Sulaf's Story: How Tranferrable Skills Lead to Career Success." Blog. 2019. https://www.wes.org/advisor-blog/transferable-skills-career-success/.

## CHAPTER 6

AAMC. "Core Competencies for Entering Medical Students." 2022. https://www.aamc.org/services/admissions-lifecycle/competencies-entering-medical-students.

Buse, Kathleen R., and Diana Bilimoria. "Personal vision: enhancing work engagement and the retention of women in the engineering profession." *Frontiers in psychology* 5 (2014): 1400.

Carlin, Barbara A., Betsy D. Gelb, Jamie K. Belinne, and Latha Ramchand. "Bridging the gender gap in confidence." *Business Horizons* 61, no. 5 (2018): 765–774.

Daly, Annemarie, David Baunoch, Kelly Rehling, Natalie Luke, Meghan Campbell, Patrick Cacdac, Miguel Penaranda et al. "Utilization of M-PCR and P-AST for diagnosis and management of urinary tract infections in home-based primary care." *JOJ Urology & Nephrology* 7, no. 2 (2020): 555707.

Josephs-Spaulding, Jonathan, Thøger Jensen Krogh, Hannah Clara Rettig, Mark Lyng, Mariam Chkonia, Silvio Waschina, Simon Graspeuntner, Jan Rupp, Jakob Møller-Jensen, and Christoph Kaleta. "Recurrent urinary tract infections: unraveling the complicated environment of uncomplicated rUTIs." *Frontiers in Cellular and Infection Microbiology* (2021): 493.

Moreno, Maria. "I usually don't rebuild panels, but I am so proud I took on." LinkedIn, March 2022. https://www.linkedin.com/feed/update/urn:li:activity:6898269303272013826/.

ROI Institute. "About Us." 2022. www.roiinstitute.net.

Riggs, Stephanie. "While at Air Liquide, my career path has been far from textbook." LinkedIn, April 2022. https://www.linkedin.com/posts/stephanie-riggs-p-e-b8464a4_ittakesavillage-leadership-success-activity-6903532557539840000-GkNP/.

## CHAPTER 7

Benson, Alan, Danielle Li, and Kelly Shue. "'Potential' and the gender promotion gap." Working paper, 2021.

Google. "Dictionary." 2022. https://www.google.com/search?q=define+hypothesis&rlz=1C1CHBF_enUS853US853&oq=define+hypothesis&aqs=chrome.69i57j0i512l9.3737j1j7&sourceid=chrome&ie=UTF-8.

Malakasis, Carol. "Can imposter syndrome in sales be a good thing?" LinkedIn, October 2021. https://www.linkedin.com/feed/update/urn:li:activity:6849331940806410241/.

## CHAPTER 8

Buse, Kathleen R., and Diana Bilimoria. "Personal vision: enhancing work engagement and the retention of women in the engineering profession." *Frontiers in psychology* 5 (2014): 1400.

Reimagining the Human Experience. "6 Phase Guided Meditation for Positive Energy." Video, 17.12 minutes. https://www.youtube.com/watch?v=p3USG9PEnWY.

## CHAPTER 10

Adhikari, B. K., Agrawal, A. and Malm, J., "Do Women Managers Keep Firms out of Trouble? Evidence from Corporate Litigation and Policies." *Journal of Accounting and Economics*, vol. 67, no. 1, pp. 202–25, 2019.

Cho, Yonjoo, et al. "'A woman CEO? You'd better think twice!': Exploring career challenges of women CEOs at multinational corporations in South Korea." *Career Development International* (2019).

Connell, Raewyn. "Gender, Health and Theory: Conceptualizing the Issue, in Local and World Perspective." *Social Science & Medicine* 74 (2012): 1675-1683.

de Luis-Carnicer, Pilar, et al. "Gender diversity in management: curvilinear relationships to reconcile findings." *Gender in Management: An International Journal* (2008).

OECD Data. "Gender Wage Gap." 2022. https://data.oecd.org/earnwage/gender-wage-gap.htm.

O'Neil, Deborah A., Margaret M. Hopkins, and Diana Bilimoria. "A framework for developing women leaders: Applications to executive coaching." *The Journal of Applied Behavioral Science* 51.2 (2015): 253-276.

Schilt, Kristen. *Just One of the Guys?: Transgender Men and the Persistence of Gender Inequality*. University of Chicago Press, 2011.

Williams, Christine L. "The glass escalator, revisited: Gender inequality in neoliberal times, SWS feminist lecturer." *Gender & Society* 27.5 (2013): 609-629.

Made in the USA
Coppell, TX
31 May 2023

17540664R00085